GHOSTS II

GHOSTS
SAN FRANCISCO

GHOSTS II

A TIME REMEMBERED

PHILIP MAKANNA

Published by GHOSTS
665 Arkansas Street, San Francisco, CA 94107

www.ghosts.com

ISBN Hardbound 0-916997-22-7

Designed by Richard Escasany, San Francisco

Printed in Hong Kong

First Edition

10 9 8 7 6 5 4 3 2 1

IN COMMEMORATION OF

THE ACHIEVEMENTS OF

THE CONFEDERATE AIR FORCE

MY SPECIAL THANKS TO COLONEL LLOYD P. NOLEN
AND COLONEL LEFTY GARDNER

THIS BOOK WOULD NOT EXIST HAD IT NOT BEEN FOR THE WARMTH OF THE MEN AND WOMEN OF THE CONFEDERATE AIR FORCE AND THE PATIENT UNDERSTANDING OF JEAN AND NICHOLAS

CONTENTS

GHOSTS II

INTRODUCTION

GHOSTS II is a recreation of the original *GHOSTS, A Time Remembered* which was published in 1979. This edition updates the original text and presents a new selection of 64 photographs. These images, a collection of personal favorites, chronicle a small part of my 25 years in the air with the Confederate Air Force.

All of the aircraft in this book were CAF aircraft when they were photographed. Several of them are the only airworthy examples of their type in existence. A few have vanished forever.

In 2002, the Confederate Air Force will change its name and a unique aviation tradition will become history. GHOSTS II is intended to be a collection of memories of a time gone by and a salute to a group of aviators who flew with a very special style.

Philip Makanna
July, 2001

I

I was born in 1940. I have the shadowed memory of a great rumbling sound. The screen door is banging and my mother is running across the lawn.

"Planes! …"

Shading her eyes and searching the sky, she is lost in the thunder that is rolling over us. She points, and I see tiny shadows in the clouds. Fighter planes are being moved to a place beyond my imagination.

Until recently, I was never closer to the planes than I was on that afternoon, but I believed, as did most of the other little boys of my generation, that the planes were magic; we dreamed and listened to stories about them with wonder. I remember hearing that at dawn on D-day, the sky was filled from horizon to horizon with black and white invasion stripes that were painted on the wings and fuselages of every plane. They were the simple, secret marking for the swarm of allied air forces that darkened the sky over the channel that day. We didn't see them, but we dreamed.

We dreamed of being test pilots and we studied silhouettes and filed blunt white-pine wings with little sandpaper paddles to make them sharp and graceful. We hung die-cast propellers on straight pins. The tiny props turned in the wind as we walked across the lawn, holding the plane overhead so that it banked majestically against the sky. We saw ourselves diving out of the sun, ducking through clouds and rolling in the sky like lazy sharks. These dreams of freedom encouraged our earthbound spirits.

The generation of men who flew in that war were our fathers. They flew through a nightmare that has become a dream. Today, as retired "snowbirds" in flight from the cold midwestern winter, they wander south in campers and RVs to the farthest tip of Texas and walk alone between rows of old planes. They have tears in their eyes. What they have seen and what they see now is a mystery I can never know.

Near the point where Texas and Mexico and the Gulf come together is an air base built in 1941. Back then, it was the site of the Harlingen Aerial Gunnery School. Hundreds of acres of concrete apron are still there, as are the huge arched hangers that were the shops for the repair of trainers and fighters and bombers. There are rows of palm trees that rustled in the Gulf wind then as they do now. There are ghosts there. I have heard them whispering near my shoulders at night as I crouched under the wings of old hospital planes that are parked out of the way, never to fly again. I have felt them over my head fluttering like moths in a steamy dawn. I have seen their shapes flickering through the blue TV light over a lonely man in a steel bunk in the Bachelor Officers Quarters.

He was here sixty years ago, during the war, when there were hundreds of people moving at every hour of the day. There were jeeps and six-bi's and tank trucks running up and down the road. Near the hangar stood a bakery and a huge mess hall. The shops were active twenty-four hours of every day. The flight line had 400 T-6s moving in and out and crews and pilots for each one. P-39s were landing as rows of B-24s stood waiting for takeoff. Men left Harlingen and went to fields all over the world and flew terrifying missions. Some came back with holes in their planes. Some didn't come back, and others lay dead or dying on runways thousands of miles from south Texas.

In 1968 the Harlingen Aerial Gunnery School became Rebel Field, headquarters of the "Ghosts Squadron" of the Confederate Air Force.

I first encountered the Confederate Air Force in September of 1976 in Reno during an air show that featured a reenactment of the Japanese attack on Pearl Harbor. From their base in Galveston, the Gulf Coast Wing of the Confederate Air Force had flown a B-17, a P-40, a P-39, and a half-dozen replica Zeros that Twentieth Century-Fox had made for the film Tora! Tora! Tora!

Soft Hawaiian music sighed over the desert as the Zeros approached in tight formation. "December 7, 1941...the time is 7:55 A.M. It is a peaceful Sunday morning near Honolulu..." balls of fire bloomed in the Nevada sand... the B-17 streamed smoke and approached a landing with only one wheel down. The P-40 and the P-39 scrambled to intercept the Zeros and defend the crippled bomber.

In a simple form that is what happened, but my memory is shot with unforgettable images among fragments of history. Pearl-gray airplanes scraped the sagebrush with rising suns as the Imperial Japanese Navy, thirty-five years out of time and place, arranged balls of red flame in a landscape of browns and dusty greens. More than 2,000 American lives had been lost at Pearl harbor in 1941 and yet, three decades later, Japanese fighter planes, specters of the enemy of the past, were flying in formation over Nevada. This time the pilots were Texans. Among them was a rancher, a pipe fitter, a crop duster, a NASA engineer. On his forehead each wore a white bandanna centered with a rising sun and the Japanese characters that signify the "Divine Wind"

In 1281 Kublai Khan sent a huge fleet across the sea to invade Japan. His success was almost insured until a wind sent by God destroyed the Chinese fleet. In 1945, young Japanese pilots wore the Rising Sun and sacrificed their lives in the belief that the Divine Wind, the Kamikaze, would deliver their homeland again. Thirty-one years later, the Rising Sun was being worn by Texans flying over a Nevada desert decorated with fire.

In the spring of 1977, haunted by what I had seen in Reno, I drove to Harlingen in south Texas to spend time at Rebel Field. As I departed, I told myself that I was going to Texas to document the activities of a group of aviators. I was to learn in the months that followed that I had gone because of my childhood dreams and the dreams of the generation of men that had inspired them.

On the way, I stopped in Dallas and visited one of the legendary pioneers of aviation in the Southwest. He showed me a worn brass card that identified him as a member of the International Order of Quiet Birdmen, an organization that dates back to the First World War.

"We are the Order of the Kiwi and the Modoc," he said. "The Kiwi is , of course, a nonflying bird. The Modoc...well, you'll have to find out about that."

After this cryptic disclosure, he put his feet up on his desk and looked at the ceiling and told me about the old days, about adventure and heroism. In those moments his eyes were wet and glistening. He said he was afraid that the old spirit would die with the men who had created it. "You'll meet men in south Texas who have that spirit and that courage. Ask them about the Kiwi and the Modoc."

II

Lloyd P. Nolen, who invented the Confederate Air Force in the late 1950's, first learned to fly in Denton, Texas, when he was fifteen years old.

"We had an old airplane," he told me, "a Cabin-Waco. It carried four passengers. In the springtime we'd fly out to east Texas and find a country town and buzz around it. People in those days knew that when they saw an airplane flying in circles it was probably trying to land and they'd drive out to see it. We'd have found a pasture someplace and made arrangements to pay the farmer ten dollars to land there all day long. When the people came out we'd take 'em for rides at all kinds of prices. That was barnstorming."

When the war started, Nolen joined the Army Air Corps. At eighteen, he had already logged 300 hours of flying time so the Air Corps Training Command grabbed him, put him on active status, and gave him the job they needed most to fill – flight instructor.

He taught flying at civilian flying schools until the end of the war. He taught glider pilots how to fly in powered airplanes on a grass patch before they went to glider school. He taught field artillery officers how to fly Piper Cubs that they called "Maytag Messerschmitts." He flew from a meadow in Terrell, Texas to train British cadets to fly Stearmans and AT-6s. He became known as a genius in an AT-6. Although he was constantly tormented by news from former students who were flying exotic planes in romantic places, he never left the United States and he never saw combat.

When the war ended, Nolen got out of the training business and into the crop-dusting business and headed south to the semitropical Rio Grande Valley. He made arrangements with the owners of a little country airport in Mercedes, and has been flying from that field ever since.

Mercedes is a very small town and the duster strip is miles from anything. There are no traffic corridors or safety hazards; instead there is the freedom of a limitless sky. A pilot can go up any day and do loops and rolls and figure-eights right over the hangars, or maybe wander out over the surf and "run the beach". No one files a flight plan when he leaves the Mercedes strip and no one worries much about what to do after he leaves the ground.

In 1951 Nolen bought a surplus P-40 Warhawk for $1,500 and his weekend exercises got more interesting. A half-dozen of his friends took turns flying the old Warhawk around the hangars of what had become known as "Rebel Field". The most popular type of flying around Mercedes was "beating up the field", a British expression describing a low-level surprise attack made at very high speed. In south Texas "beating up the field" was – and still is – a sport witnessed by the wise from a prone position. On any Sunday, spectators skitter from hangar to bush as enthusiastic pilots keep the grass trimmed.

Lloyd sold the P-40 in 1952 to buy a faster and more powerful P-51 Mustang. The gas tank of a Mustang could be removed from the fuselage and replaced with a passenger seat that doubled the fun. But the Korean conflict had begun and the Air Force recalled all of its surplus Mustangs and repurchased most of those that were in civilian hands. It was five years before another P-51 was available. In 1957 Nolen located a Mustang in El Paso. It had a chewed-up tailpiece as the result of an altercation with a light plane, but it was repairable and Nolen flew it home. The $2,500 price tag was split between Nolen and four neighbors.

The five partners rolled the airplane out one fine Sunday and found that someone had stolen into the hangar by the light of the moon and painted CONFEDERATE AIR FORCE on the fuselage below the tail. That sounded sort of good and the name stuck. So, next thing you know, Nolen and the boys started saluting one another... then two of them commissioned each other Colonel, and the other three declared themselves Sergeants. Pretty soon the

Sergeants decided that since they owned the airplane equally, they damn well should be Colonels, too. It was decreed that, thenceforth, "everyone in this air force is a Colonel," and that stuck, too. Today, in 2001, the Confederate Air Force has one hundred forty-seven aircraft and a membership of more than 9000.

It was not long before the Colonels realized that they couldn't dogfight with one airplane and they started looking for another World War II fighter. The logical mate for a Mustang was a Bearcat, a Grumman F8F, which during it's service career held the record for rate of climb and was the fastest and most powerful prop-driven Navy fighter.

Lefty Gardner, Lloyd's next-door neighbor, reminisced about Nolen's second acquisition as we sipped his wife Sharon's enlightening beet wine to the tune of midnight sugarcane trucks howling past the Mercedes airstrip.

"One day the Navy called up and said, 'You want your Bearcats, Double-LP?' Lloyd said, 'What Bearcats?' The Navy said, 'The two you bid eight hundred and five dollars for. You won them. If you want them, get yourself out to Litchfield Park in Arizona and fly them kittys out of here.'

"So Lloyd went to Phoenix and spent all day long looking over thirty-two Bearcats that were filled with red sand and had been sitting derelict in hundred-and-ten degree heat for ten years. The Commander at the base said, "You get one of those airplanes out of here TODAY, 'cause we're fixin' to close this space and melt those Bearcats down." About four fifty-nine the Commander walked back out and said, 'When are you fixin' to leave with your Bearcat?' Lloyd told him, 'Well I'm fixin to leave just as soon as I can figure out how to get in and crank it up.' The Commander said, 'Well, you push that button right there and you can open the canopy and get in. Then punch that shiny button right there and fire it up and LEAVE here! Now, when you leave, don't you EVER come back!' So Lloyd said, 'Okay. Adios,' and the commander turned on his heel and left.

"Lloyd pushed all the shiny buttons and the plane fired up, so he taxied out to the end of the runway. He then proceeded to take off... and pushed another button and the gear came up. He got up about two thousand feet and the engine quit. He was probably figuring to himself, "I expect I ought to go back and land at the base 'cause it's a little smoother back there than it is out here.' So he did a hundred-and-eighty-degree turn and lit back to the base and the Commander came roarin' out and said "I thought I told you not to come back to this base once you left here.' Lloyd said, 'Well, Commander, I thought I could negotiate with you better than I could with those sand dunes, so I came back.'

"The Base Commander said, 'Well, okay. Here are some

new spark plugs. You put 'em in right now and depart again.' About three days, forty-eight plugs, several mechanics, and mucho cerveza later, Lloyd took off and headed for El Paso."

As Lefty tells it, it took three weeks and a multitude of romantic aeronautical maneuvers in 100-degree heat before the Colonel and his Bearcat arrived home at "Rebel Field", Mercedes. The second Bearcat was retrieved a few weeks later. The remaining F8Fs were dragged to the smelter and destroyed.

The Confederate Air Force now had three airplanes and five Colonels. When the Naval Air Station at Kingsville asked them to demonstrate the Mustang and the Bearcat at their airshow in 1960, they were genuinely surprised. The CAF Colonels thought the new jets were the glamorous way to fly, but they soon learned that they weren't glamorous to those who flew them. The early jets were under-powered. They had huge appetites for fuel and limited capacities for carrying it. This made predetermined flight plans a necessity. Freedom was becoming a thing of the past. After the airshow, Navy pilots came out to the flight-line at sunset, crawled up inside the old warbirds and dreamed of flying behind huge four-blade propellers…of boring holes in the clouds. It was a dream that would be hard to forget.

Lefty Gardner was in his early twenties during the war. He flew forty-three missions – thirteen of them as "tail-end Charlie" – piloting a B-17 over Germany. In 1950 Gardner originated airborne brush control in west Texas and became something of a legend as the Cowboy Aviator. "Flyin' mesquite," as Gardner termed his version of crop-dusting, required dramatic aerial flip-flops over the vast areas of range that make up the Panhandle ranches. To achieve greater maneuverability, he customized his Stearman bi-planes with special high-lift wings that allowed them to drift down the sides of cliffs and climb out of canyons hanging on the propeller.

Lefty met Lloyd Nolen in 1960. Gardner was living north of Laredo and was in the market for radial motors for his Stearmans. They were very scarce at the time but he located several and, to check on them, called Nolen who told him to forget about the ones he had found and, instead, fly with him to Canada "to get the same engines with airplanes attached." Lloyd Nolen had a sharp eye for the makings of a Colonel and the Confederate Air Force began the induction of Lefty Gardner.

"The next thing I knew," Gardner remembers, "Lloyd was flying us up to Crystal City through lightning and thunderclouds blacker'n the inside of a cow. Of course, I should have known that there was something fishy about a guy who would fly through weather like that just to pick me up to take me to Canada to get a good deal on a couple of engines. When Lloyd came, he brought all the pilots he had, so I rounded up all the pilots I had and we flew to Canada. We landed at Lethbridge, Alberta, at an abandoned air base and when we flung open the door of the hangar there was a bunch of T-6s scattered all over the floor. They didn't have engines on 'em or radios in 'em. They didn't even have wings on 'em. But, I knew that we had found some low-time airplanes and if we could get 'em back to Texas we'd be able to fly the heck out of 'em – and then sell 'em for a fortune.

"For two or three days we talked to a lawyer and Lloyd talked to me about the Confederate Air Force. He told me about the thrill of flying a Mustang and a Bearcat and about how much more fun those fighters were to fly than a Stearman or a bomber – all that kind of stuff.

"We finally got our T-6s put together and spun 'em back to Texas and Lloyd put me in the back seat of the Mustang and flew me around the hangars and showed me the Bearcat, which, according to him is a much better plane than the Mustang. My blood pressure was ninety-five over seventy and I was ready to go. So he said, 'I happen to know that there's a Corsair out in Buckeye, Arizona. Why don't you go get it?"

Thus did Lloyd snare Lefty, an innocent li'l ol' crop-duster from Crystal City, Texas. In years to come, rusty wrecks were located in swamps and snow banks all over North and South America and Europe. They were flown, often at great risk, to south Texas. They were restored and the Confederate Air Force grew.

In the spring of 1962 the mythical Colonel Jethro E. Culpeper, phantom Commander of the CAF, whose directives are conveyed by his Deputy, Colonel L. P. Nolen, awarded Colonel Gardner the Silver Magnolia Blossom (Heroic) for the recovery of the CAF's first P-38. Lefty and his brother, Colonel Henry Gardner, had flown to Hayward, California, to retrieve a Hellcat. Lefty had acquired the P-38 in the process. The citation describing the task and skills that distinguished the new Colonel, (formerly an innocent li'l ol' crop duster from Crystal City, Texas) reads in part:

...LEFTY GARDNER, 60-110, COLONEL, CONFEDERATE AIR FORCE, FOR GALLANTRY IN ACTION IN THE HEROIC ACHIEVEMENT AND AT GREAT PERSONAL RISK, IN CONNECTION WITH MILITARY OPERATIONS OVER YANKEE STRONGHOLDS IN THE VICINITY OF CALIFORNIA, ARIZONA, AND FLORIDA, DID, UNDER EXTREME AND ADVERSE CONDITIONS, ACHIEVE THE FOLLOWING:

EARLY ON THE MORNING OF 10 SEPTEMBER 1961, WEARY-EYED FROM POISONOUS YANKEE WHISKEY AND FROM THWARTING THE NIGHTLONG ATTACK OF A DAMNYANKEE SPY,

Col. Gardner managed to find his way to Sacramento Airport to take delivery of one P-38 aircraft on behalf of the Confederate Air Force and deliver said aircraft to CAF Headquarters, Rebel Field, Texas. Upon completion of the transaction and acceptance, Col. Gardner discovered that all maintenance manuals, and operations instructions had been stolen by Yankee spies. This would have been a devastating blow to a lesser man; however, Col. Gardner immediately deduced that since this aircraft had two engines and two tails, he simply would do everything as in other aircraft except he would do it two times. Colonel Gardner seated himself in this great flying machine, surveyed the cockpit, and determined the use and purpose of each and every lever and switch, except four, stowed his gear in some proper place, started the engines, roared down the runway and into the blue of the California sky and headed for DIXIE...

...While crossing the Sierra Mountains, Col. Gardner found that his main fuel tank had become filled with air. At this point, the engines pulled a typical Yankee trick – they quit. With utmost dispatch and cool logic and determination, Col. Gardner moved all switches and valves until the engines again began to function. Having surmounted these difficulties he was then able to locate the State of Arizona....

As he moved across the Texas border, a strong Texas tailwind began to impede his progress to the degree that even though his indicated airspeed was 272 mph it took him one hour and eighty-two minutes to fly from El Paso to Midland, a distance of 250 miles.
After landing and gassing at Midland, Col. Gardner, due to his superior intelligence and skillful airmanship, calculated that the cause of his low ground speed was the fact that this strong tailwind had blown his flaps down. With this successfully corrected, he sailed into Rebel Field, undaunted by the fact that his wife shook her fist at him as he passed over his home at Crystal City, having been gone only one week and nine days on a three-day trip.

This being his third and least hazardous ferrying experience with the Confederate Air Force, having previously brought an FG-1D Corsair from the dust of Arizona and a P-40 Warhawk from the swamps of Florida, Col. Gardner was not in the least shook-up by such mild

AND MINOR MISCALCULATIONS. THE CIA (CONFEDERATE INTELLIGENCE AGENCY) HAS CLASSIFIED THE FLORIDA AND ARIZONA FLIGHT TOP SECRET. IT CAN BE REVEALED, HOWEVER, THAT IN THE CASE OF THE P-40, COL. GARDENER ASCERTAINED THAT SABOTEURS HAD STOLEN THE PITCH OUT OF HIS PROP AND THE COB OUT OF HIS CARBURETOR AND THE GIN OUT OF HIS GENERATOR. IN THE CASE OF THE CORSAIR, IT WAS OBVIOUS THAT SOMEONE HAD PUT THE WINGS ON UPSIDE DOWN....

...HIS ACTIONS WILL DO MUCH TO FAMILIARIZE THIS AND COMING GENERATIONS WITH THESE GREAT FIGHTING AIRCRAFT AS WELL AS WITH THE SUPERIOR MILITARY JUDGEMENT, TACTICAL SKILL, AND TREMENDOUS PERSONAL COURAGE OF THIS GREAT REBEL. THE HIGH QUALITIES OF JUDGEMENT, COURAGE, AND DEVOTION TO DUTY DISPLAYED BY COL. GARDNER, AND THE FACT THAT HE GOT HERE A-TALL, REFLECTS GREAT CREDIT UPON HIMSELF AND THE CONFEDERATE AIR FORCE.

By 1963 the CAF had acquired each of the ten American fighter planes from World War II: a North American P-51 Mustang, a Republic P-47 Thunderbolt, a Chance Vought FG-1D Corsair, a Curtiss P-40 Warhawk, a Grumman F4F Wildcat (General Motors FM-2), a Lockheed P-38 Lightning, a Bell P-39 Aircobra, a Grumman F8F Bearcat, a Grumman F6F Hellcat and a Bell P-63 Kingcobra.

The Colonels then began looking for World War II American bombers. They found a B-25 Mitchell, a medium bomber, and an A-26 Invader, an attack bomber and night fighter, and flew them successfully from the strip at Mercedes. A Douglas A-20 Havoc, a twin-engined light bomber, was tracked down, and , in 1967, a Martin B-26 medium bomber was located in Denver.

The activity in the air on Sundays in Mercedes was becoming famous, and Rebel Field could not accommodate the crowds that the airshows attracted. Parked cars and pickup trucks slowed traffic for miles around the duster strip. The Colonels were beginning to talk about expanding their collection to include the "heavies" – maybe a B-17 Flying Fortress or a B-24 Liberator – but the 2,900 foot runway at Mercedes was too short and had too light a base to support a heavy bomber.

In 1968 the city of Harlingen offered the CAF a new home at the former Harlingen Aerial Gunnery School. The Colonels moved their headquarters fourteen miles east and christened the World War II base "Rebel Field". Mercedes became "Old Rebel Field".

Shortly thereafter the CAF took delivery of a B-17 and a B-24 that had been in service for Petroleos Mexicano, the Mexican national oil company. The big bombers had been resident at Lefty Gardner's base in Brownwood, Texas. Brownwood city officials had decided that they were less than desirable.

Negotiations for a Spitfire began. Messerschmitts and a Heinkel were found in Spain. In 1970, a B-29 was located in the California desert, where it had been standing since 1954 and was scheduled to be a target for ballistic missile tests. A pilot flying over the China Lake Ordinance Depot, spotted the huge silver silhouette while it was still a fugitive from naval rockets. A crew of CAF mechanics and pilots headed by Lefty Gardner was soon deployed and spent nine weeks in the desert working on the Superfortress. On August 3, 1971 – for the first time in seventeen years – the old bomber slowly lifted itself from the floor of the Mojave Desert. It flew nonstop to Harlingen in six hours and thirty-eight minutes.

Near Ontario, California, the Colonels located a Curtiss SB2C Helldiver, the ponderous "Big-tailed Beast" that had been the standard carrier-based dive bomber at the end of the war. It stood on rotting tires, at the end of a runway in Chino. Every window in its canopy was broken and pigeons had been roosting in its cockpits for ten years. A detachment of bats hung in the gloom behind the tail gunner's harness and, further down, the shadows had spawned the largest colony of black widow spiders north of Acapulco. Colonel Bob Griffin became sponsor of the SB2C and dispatched two Confederate mechanics to the Coast with a truck and a trailer to restore it and fly it home. One year later, piloted by Colonel Gerald Martin, the "Beast" flew back to Texas, becoming the only airworthy Helldiver of the 6,000 that were built.

In 1971, Colonel Ed Jurist bought a DeHavilland Mosquito in England. Prized by the Royal Air Force pilots for its versatility, the "Mossie" flew higher and faster than most other world War II fighters. This was largely due to the fact that, except for its two Rolls-Royce engines, It was made of plywood. In December of 1971, Colonels Jurist and Duane Egli flew the Mosquito from London to the Azores and then across the North Atlantic to Newfoundland. In London, Colonel Egli had replaced camshafts in both engines, overhauled both carburetors, overhauled four magnetos, and removed a bird's nest from the right main fuel cell. Navigation and communications radios had failed over the coast of Spain in a shower of sparks and the "Mossie" had scattered most of its exhaust stacks across the Atlantic. On the second of January, 1972, they landed the thirty-one-year-old plywood frame at Rebel Field, climaxing an extraordinary period of CAF aircraft recovery. At this point, the Confederate Air Force had accumulated fifty-six aircraft.

The maintenance of the Confederate Air Force aircraft is an enormous task. Most of the airplanes are something like sixty years old and the FAA regularly inspects each one to ensure that all are maintained to standards. The annual inspection of the B-29 requires 288 hours of labor – nine days for a crew of four. Fifty miles of tubing and cables are checked, as are the 342 functions of the landing gear and the hydraulic and electrical systems. One hundred and five functions are checked in each of the four engines and 144 spark plugs and 340 gallons of oil are changed.

Many parts are now unavailable. Although Confederate Air Force hangars are filled with crates of exotic bits and pieces that solve a lot of problems, the extensive stock of equipment manufactured in the forties is disappearing piece by piece, bit by bit. Every part has a finite life and when a piston burns, a cam wears flat, or a cylinder head cracks, there may be no replacement available. New parts must be specially built or custom-made to fit the requirement.

The CAF's mechanical ingenuity was demonstrated to me in Harlingen on a wet summer morning in 1977. The FAA had grounded the F-82 Twin Mustang immediately after it had landed at Rebel Field in 1969. To get it flying again, a complicated rebuild was necessary. Of late, the task had become the pet project of Colonel Malcolm Russell, one of the geniuses of the CAF's staff of mechanics. After many months of creative tinkering, Russell had gotten the Rolls-Royce Merlin V-12 engines in running order and had solved a critical mechanical problem by adapting the brake drums from another airplane to the Twin Mustang's system.

It was a special morning for Colonel Russell. When the rain stopped at eight-thirty, he carefully towed the big twin-engined fighter from its hangar, pulled each prop to a precisely vertical position and fussed in the cockpit for a minute. Then, alone in the little yellow tug, he raced out across the concrete apron dodging and splashing through puddles that had formed in the pre-dawn rain. Colonel Gardner climbed into the cockpit about nine-thirty. The mechanics assembled on the wing for a conference and then everybody moved back. Gardner pushed buttons, the Merlin's coughed smoke, fire ballooned out of the stacks, and both engines caught. Russell moved close behind the huge spinning blades and leaned on the prop wash. Holding a tubular frame member, he pulled himself off his feet, reached up and put the flat of his hand into the exhaust as it came out of each of the twenty-four stacks. Because of the terrible roar of the engines the best way to tell if every cylinder is firing is to feel the heat of each exhaust. Gardner revved a motor – blue fire smacked Russell's palm and the prop wash nearly blew him into the wing. Gardner shut the motors down and Colonel Russell's feet came back to earth.

He climbed the wing to confer with Gardner. He was grinning. Thumbs up! It had been a critical and successful test session. The little flags of hair that remain on the sides of his head were standing back like Mercury's wings. Soon afterward, the Twin Mustang flew for the first time in eight years and became the only airworthy F-82 in the world.

III

When I arrived in Harlingen in May of 1977, I checked into a motel on the Sunshine Strip and waited a few days to hear from Colonel Lloyd Nolen. I had already spoken to Colonel Nolen, who had been introduced to me as the Colonel in Charge of Literary Affairs, about the book I hoped write about the Confederate Air Force. Finally, Nolen agreed to meet me and invited me to join him for dinner. When he arrived at the door of my motel room, Nolen first encountered my dog, Pal, a friendly terrier of various breeding. He studied Pal for a long and serious moment, and then he spoke, more to himself than to me, "A guy with a dog like that couldn't be all bad."

After he stepped inside Colonel Nolen addressed a few polite words to me and then regarded Pal for a long stretch. We, all three, fidgeted a little. Colonel Nolen was concerned about the sincerity of the stranger who stood before him with the smiling dog. Pal's wisdom was apparent, but the project proposed by his master was not to be taken lightly and there was always the possibility that the dog was just a front.

His next words were, "Offhand, I'd say he's a trick dog."

Fortunately, he said this with warmth and the awkwardness between us vanished. Pal became an unofficial Colonel in the Confederate Air Force. His photograph was hung in the headquarters building at Rebel field. I have no doubt that it was because of him that I was invited to fly in a number of extraordinary airplanes, piloted by some very extraordinary men.

They say John Huston kept a dumb old horse in his barn for the initiation of strangers and that when anyone but Huston climbed aboard, the dumb old horse became a dragon. A wise man would say, "Thank you, Mr. Huston, but I think I won't ride that dumb old horse today."

I flew with lefty Gardner in his Mustang for half an hour one afternoon when I was still a newcomer to the Confederate Air force. I should have remembered the story about Huston's horse. We went down the dusty Mercedes strip and I felt the gear come in just a few feet off the ground. Next thing I new, we were pointed straight up and the right wing was straight down. Then the whole damn thing was straight down and we buzzed Old Rebel Field below the roof of the hangar. After that, distinct memory escapes me. I remember going straight up into the blue sky and thin clouds. We rolled at the top of that loop and I saw the earth swing over my head. There was no sense of falling; not a sharp or jarring movement. The Mustang gained altitude and we bored graceful holes in the clouds.

Then Lefty decided to come in low around the side of the hangar with a wing in the grass. We were upside down at least once and sideways a lot. He said he was scouting for rattlesnakes. He did a few eight-point rolls, banging the wings precisely to their stops like a snappy British salute. From time to time, he stretched around and peeked at me with one eye. I was told later that he has dropped the landing gear of his P-38 in the middle of a roll when he was only a few feet off the ramp. He has made rooster tails with his wheels in the Rio Grande. I figure I got off easy. Next time out, I decided I would ride on my back so I could see the ground.

We landed. Grinning faces came out of hiding places behind the bushes and confused cows. Old Bob Maxwell, who flew a bomber over Germany on his eighteenth birthday, climbed out on the wing of the Mustang with a fuel hose, mumbling and laughing to himself after hearing Lefty's landing request: "We'll take seventy-five gallons, Sir. Just charge that to the Army."

Since that day I have flown in B-17s and B-25s, a BT-13, a hundred AT-6s, a replica Kate torpedo bomber, T-34s, T-28s, a Dauntless, a Helldiver, too many Mustangs, and a Stearman rigged to fly under barbed-wire fences. Those flights originated from grass patches, desert air bases, commercial airports, and everything in between.

Sounds I heard in my first days in south Texas will be in my ears forever: the smooth, whistling bellow of the twin Allison V-12s in a P-38, the nasty rap from the short exhaust stacks of the Mustangs, the deep boom of the big Navy radials. I slept to the howls and rattles of a rusty air conditioner that drew the gulf wind in and left it damp and clammy.

These days I use two 35mm. Nikon F-4 cameras with Nikkor lenses. I carry a Nikon F100 with a short lens as a backup. I learned that the best way to deal with the huge space of the airfields was to spread all of my equipment in the trunk of my car between the folds of a bunched-up blanket and drive from shot to shot. I am absolutely in love with flying but I must admit that flying upside down with some of the Colonels is hard on my stomach. I feel poorly all too frequently… but I always try to smile when the Colonel glances over his shoulder at me. As this can encourage the Colonel who is doing the flips, I do my best to stay out of that back seat.

The United States Air Force invited the Confederate Air Force to participate in an airshow at the Selfridge Air National Guard base near Detroit on July 4, 1977, to celebrate the sixtieth anniversary of the base that was the military's first training field.

I joined the veteran Colonels as guests of the new generation of airmen. Colonel Ed Messick, Operations Officer, held his usual rowdy but efficient briefing before the airshow. He wore the official gray Confederate hat and carried a softball bat for a swagger stick. The young Air Force pilots were crowded into the rear of the briefing room and watched in silent amazement while Colonel Messick was cheered and booed as he called out the coming day's events.

In the middle of the briefing, Colonel Jim Hill, who, as a member of the American Volunteer Group in the late thirties, flew a "gooney bird over the hump" (a C-47 transport over the Himalayas into China), rose slowly and began to mutter something about getting out to his airplane "They're coming….They're coming….Get me to the flight line…." Then the beloved, craggy Colonel turned, slumped, and fell over the row of seats in front of him. His head was down. He was coughing and holding his chest as he sagged to the floor. For a moment his feet were up in the air. He came down like a wet towel.

Messick called for oxygen. Then, still clutching his softball bat, he collapsed on the floor too. CAF doctors jumped up and rushed to Hill's side. His cracked, veined hands trembled as they rose and fell behind the seats several times. Members of the CAF pulled him from between the seats. The young U.S. airmen arrived with oxygen. The room was silent and frozen for the moment.

Messick was standing again. He had a can of beer in his hand. He popped it, sprinkled some on Colonel Hill, and pronounced, "He'll be all right. He just needs his beer and his airplane!"

At this, Jim Hill leapt to his feet. He clapped his hands over his head, hopped around, and proclaimed his victory. The assembled Colonels cheered. The young Air Force men wobbled to the back of the hall, Messick straightened his Stetson, raised the softball bat, and sent us out into the sunshine. The young Air Force pilots left the windowless room rigid and amazed… relieved that the briefing was over.

IV

In early September of 1977 I flew to El Paso to meet Colonel Messick to fly with him to Phoenix for the CAF's Labor Day Airshow. At the briefing in El Paso, Messick scheduled the takeoffs so that all of the aircraft would meet over Phoenix at the same time. The Zeros were airborne first because they had to stop for fuel at the halfway point and then, one by one, the old planes took to the air. Messick took off last. I was his passenger.

Messick's P-51 is a trick model with auxiliary fuel cells in the wing that allow him to stay in the air for eight hours. The canopy is tinted. The cockpit is customized and plush. Any sharp edge is covered with leather and both seats are upholstered in tuck-and-roll red flannel. I expected a walnut bar to pop out of the floor.

I polished the canopy to clear the view for my camera and shoved a half-dozen anti-static wipers into the map pocket for future use. I expected that I might get fingerprints inside the bubble as we flew and I wanted to be prepared to rub them off. I stuffed my cameras and myself into the rear seat. I put on the shoulder harness and a seatbelt and was enveloped by the leather all around me. The back seat of a Mustang is no place for someone who likes to get out of airplanes fast. The sign says, "Sit down. Strap in. Shut up."

I observed Colonel Messick (as described in his Citation for the Order of the Brass Jackass) pull on his "helmet, goggles, push-button watch, buckle-over shoes, silk scarf, and leap lightly into the cockpit. Waving to the crowd in the manner of Smilin' Jack and Tailspin Tommy, he adjusted his goggles, engaged the starting lever, and the mighty Merlin roared to life."

A Mustang has a 1,500-horsepower engine, with two banks of six cylinders in line. It starts in a cloud of smoke and fire that bursts out of the little stacks and is blown back past the cockpit by a rush of air off the propeller. There is a tremendous amount of noise and vibration.

A Mustang is a tail dragger and the engine housing extends so high and far in front that there is no way of seeing straight ahead when the plane is at rest on the ground. Messick zigzagged down the length of the taxiway, looking out this side and then the other to see where he was going. We lined up next to a P-47 and Messick turned up the wick. There was an explosion of noise and wind and the plane skipped into the air. In formation off our right wing, the huge P-47 "Jug" folded its gear and climbed fast behind us.

We flew for an hour before we made contact with the

flight. I spotted a C-47 first. It was a thousand feet below us, its polished skin slashing the New Mexico sun. Then, higher and to the north, I saw the B-17, the B-24, and then the gracefully monstrous B-29. Over the headset Messick offered to come in close for pictures. I learned that "come in close" means "come in close sideways," "come in close upside down," "come in close on the top side of a barrel roll." The upside down photographer with one eye on the camera and the other eye searching for ground in zero gravity is an unhappy boy. Somewhere between a whifferdill and a Beauregard flip, my lunch got in the way of my trigger finger. Grabbing for the anti-static wipers at the bottom of the cockpit but wishing I had one of those nice doggie bags so graciously provided by the airlines, I noticed long pieces of black fur wisping over the red leather. I hauled myself up and, peering into the seat ahead, discovered that my pilot had pulled a rubber monkey face over his head and was making primate gestures at the crew of the B-24.

All of the planes gathered in orbit over Phoenix International Raceway and joined formation. Led by the "Tora Bunch" – a dozen Japanese Zeros, Kates, and Val torpedo bombers – we flew low over suburban Phoenix.

It was 120 degrees at that altitude, and because Colonel Messick was running the show and had those dandy eight-hour tanks, we were the last to land. I think that was the sickest I have ever been in my life.

The temperature on the flight line in Phoenix over the Labor Day weekend of 1977 got jammed at 125 degrees for two days. On the first day there were 350 cases of heat prostration. On the second day everyone carried an umbrella for protection from the sun.

First there was the national anthem... then, for two hours, CAF aircraft took to the air to reenact scenarios from the war... Spain in 1936, the Battle of Britain, Pearl Harbor, the North African campaign, Ploesti, Normandy, and Hiroshima. Solo aerobatics performed by Colonel Gerald Martin in a Wildcat and by Colonel Lefty Gardner in his P-38 provided intermissions between battle sequences.

The heat was unbearable as I crossed the runway with Colonels Bill McCoy and Al Jenkins to prepare the dynamite that simulates bomb bursts for the battles. We loaded explosives from steel and concrete blockhouses into pickup trucks and strung wire over the desert from blasting caps to breaker boxes. We placed gray plastic pails full of gasoline on top of the explosives and topped them off with crankcase oil. It was a slow, dangerous job that demanded order and delicacy.

There was no more than a moment of rest before the Zeros appeared. They came in just a few feet off the Arizona sand and our fire began boiling 100 feet into the hot air. Across the shimmering runway, a mirage of 50,000 silent people stood with black umbrellas over their heads.

Ghosts were all around me. The Zeros came in... "December 7, 1941"... and I was just feet away as they passed and the air writhed and shrieked and tore itself in turbulent aftershock. I turned and saw a P-40 painted with the jaws of a Flying Tiger skim into the dream...the teeth of the shark...the phantom mouth of Death. I stood and stumbled through clouds of oily smoke. I was hammered by hot concussions as the fuel vaporized and boiled into the sky. I had strayed into a level of Hell. The moment froze and I wandered with spirits from another time.

The events at Phoenix and at other airshows around the country are part of a ceremony created by a generation of men who saw the ritual as reality some sixty years ago. They experienced the edge that defines life; they saw their friends pass over the brink and not return. They lived through the tragedy as only they can know. The eternal is of no consequence to them because they have flirted with the Angel of Death.

V

Dawn is a moment that aviators consider enchanted. It provides a door to the unknown. As the sun nears the edge of the horizon it creates a silent aura of magic – birds and animals pause. First light imparts a calm to the air and to those who would fly into it.

Except for the un-restored hospital planes that stand forgotten at the back of the ramp, the flight line of the Harlingen Aerial Gunnery School is deserted at dawn most of the year. But in October, for four mornings, men move quietly on the concrete in the darkness before the sunrise. Motors start in the gloom and the planes rise through the mist and fly out over a lacework of green and brown to rendezvous over the Gulf. A squadron of ghosts – Avengers, Wildcats, Hellcats, Bearcats, Mustangs, Warhawks, Zeros, Thunderbolts, Lightnings... a Helldiver, a Dauntless, a Flying Fortress, a Liberator... they fly in formation over a silent sea as the sun cracks the darkened sky.

On one of these mornings I flew with Colonel Larry Irvine in the SBD Dauntless, the Navy's best dive-bomber in the early years of the war. The Dauntless was old when the war began. Its design dates to 1934. From the open canopy I could see its round-headed rivets protruding from the wing like navy-blue bubbles. As we drifted alone through the warm, damp air, a B-25 bomber crossed the sky overhead and then, diving down over our left wing, disappeared. A P-40, a Messerschmitt, and a Hellcat followed in flashes. They flew out of the sunrise toward a steaming south Texas landscape and the palm trees of the Harlingen Aerial Gunnery School.

We followed an Avenger out over the Gulf that morning. We never got very close. It remained some distance away and then disappeared into the gold reflected by the sea. We dropped low over the beach, flew for miles just a few feet off the waves, and returned to base. It was a beautiful morning and a beautiful flight. I had not made a single photograph. I guess I never felt the need to.

On an overcast evening in Harlingen, Colonel Bob Maxwell took my arm and led me away from the hangars. We walked hundreds of yards until we were near the center of the huge concrete ramp. There was nothing out there except an occasional recess that hides the steel eyes used to tie down T-6s flown during the war. As an explanation, Maxwell told me that I needed to see "Hines's name". He pointed to the concrete near where we stood and I read "H-I-N-E-S" written in tar. Maxwell had been there when Hines had written his name on the runway in 1943. In 1945, Maxwell learned that Hines, a gunner in a B-17, had been killed somewhere in Europe. He was silent for a moment; then he continued. He told me that, during the war, crewmen stood alone at their positions across the vast ramp. They dug the sun-softened tar out of the cracks that separated the slabs and dabbed their marks on the concrete. As we walked away slowly, I saw around me the initials "T.L.," and the name "Jo," "D.J.M." with a square around it, the words "Hawaii" and "Texas." When I drew back, I could see hundreds of names and marks and symbols across the concrete. I remembered that Native Americans tapped the flat faces of cliffs with small rocks and made indelible marks and symbols at important locations – at crossroads or where canyons narrowed. We call them petroglyphs. In similar fashion, Hines and the other men knew that they stood at a cross road and they made their mark in a nearly indestructible medium.

HINES

It began to rain. Colonel Maxwell and I went to the end of the ramp and took
shelter under the wing of one of the hospital planes. Lightning flared all around us. I made one photograph.

"REBEL FIELD" - HARLINGEN, TEXAS 1976

NORTH AMERICAN AT-6A TEXAN

USS RANGER
VF-41
CONFEDERATE AIR FORCE
41-F-4

NAKAJIMA B5N KATES, AICHI D3A VALS (REPLICAS)

EII-142

CURTISS P-40N WARHAWK

MITSUBISHI A6M2 ZEROS, NAKAJIMA B5N KATES, AICHI D3A VALS (REPLICAS)

MITSUBISHI A6M2 ZEROS (REPLICAS), CURTISS P-40N WARHAWK

AICHI D3A VALS (REPLICAS)

GRUMMAN FM-2 (F4F) WILDCATS

CONSOLIDATED PBY-5A CATALINA

CONFEDERATE AIR FORCE
ZK-TEX
K
447506
Mobil

BEECH C-45 EXPEDITER

CURTISS C-46F COMMANDO

中國空軍

HEINKEL He111 (CASA-2.111)

SUPERMARINE SPITFIRE LF Mk.IXc

MESSERSCHMITT Me109 (HA-1112-M1L), SUPERMARINE SPITFIRE LF Mk.IXc

D
B
MK297

BELL P-39Q AIRACOBRA

BELL P-63F KINGCOBRA

NORTH AMERICAN P-51D MUSTANG

GRUMMAN F8F-2 BEARCAT

REPUBLIC P-47N THUNDERBOLT

2-B-4

DOUGLAS SBD-5 (A-24B) DAUNTLESS

309
309
309

CURTISS SB2C-5 HELLDIVER

NORTH AMERICAN P-82B TWIN MUSTANG

LOCKHEED P-38J LIGHTNING

NORTH AMERICAN B-25J MITCHELL

NORTH AMERICAN B-25J (PBJ) MITCHELL

DOUGLAS A-20G HAVOC

DOUGLAS A-26B INVADER

A
4435643
Daisy Mae

DOUGLAS A-26B INVADER

MARTIN B-26C MARAUDER

NORTH AMERICAN B-25J MITCHELL

U
483514
F

L
483872
X
X
VP

90018
DIAMOND
'LIL'

BOEING TB-29A SUPERFORTRESS

BOEING TB-29A SUPERFORTRESS

BOEING TB-29A SUPERFORTRESS

GUNFIGHTER

201

GRUMMAN F6F-5 HELLCAT

EII-102

BOEING B-17G FLYING FORTRESS

FUNDAMENTALS OF AIR FIGHTING

Fundamentals of Air Fighting, a restricted pamphlet issued by the Adjutant General's Office of the War Department and published by the United states Government Printing Office in 1942, was distributed to fighter and bomber pilots in the early days of World War II.

FOREWORD

The information contained in the following pages has been derived from official and accurate reports of actual air combats and operations. Much of what is repeated here is as old as air fighting itself. The information portrayed is disseminated not as inflexible rules or directives, but rather imparts something of what has been learned of air operations thus far. It is meant to encourage initiative and study of the subjects covered by all flying personnel. The air fighter must be constantly awake to all developments, be ever alert to use his best talents to meet the ever fast moving panorama of air warfare. To anticipate future developments one must have some knowledge of past and present methods.

GUNNERY PRINCIPLES

IN AIR COMBAT, the purpose of the fighter pilot and flexible gunners, is to destroy the enemy quickly with the minimum amount of ammunition. This can best be accomplished by developing superior fire power, and firing at decisive range, which depends on:

- Accuracy of gun siting,
- Number and type of guns and amount of ammunition available,
- Correct estimation of range,
- Concentration of fire power.

Concentration of fire power may be considered in two parts, viz:

Concentration of fire in time and space depending upon the number of guns that can be brought to bear either from a single aircraft or from a formation;

Bullet density built up during fire, depending on time and range.

The area of space covered by the fire from a single gun is termed the "bullet group" for that gun.

The primary consideration is to obtain a bullet density which is likely to destroy the expected target.

The total "lethal area" of a target is the sum of the various small vulnerable or vital areas in the target in which it is probable that one bullet would result in disabling or destroying one target aircraft.

Bullet density, and the size of the bullet group are directly proportional to range, i.e., the diameter of the group at 400 yards is four times that at 100 yards.

It is imperative, in air combat, that a lethal density be built up quickly because –

- The opportunities for accurate shooting are short,
- The quicker the lethal density is built up the less likely you are to be shot down yourself.
- Increased lethal density can be built up by –
- Higher rate of gunfire,
- Increased number of guns,
- Mutual support between two or more aircraft,
- Reduction of range,
- Increased caliber of guns.

AIR FIGHTING PRINCIPLES

A FUNDAMENTAL of all air fighting tactics is simplicity and flexibility.

Tactics must be simple because of the time factor. The speed of modern aircraft does not admit of the development of elaborate formations and attacks. Other factors which demand simplicity are –

Difficulty of control,

Limited vision,

Difficulties of intercommunication,

Fleeting opportunity for decisive air combat,

Necessity of exploitation of varying weather conditions so as to effect surprise, viz: clouds, sun, haze, dawn, and dusk lighting effects.

Another fundamental affecting fighting tactics is MORALE and LEADERSHIP. A high morale is essential. It is dependent upon physical fitness, environment, a contented frame of mind and good leadership.

The leader must possess initiative and skill to judge when and from which direction maximum fire should be brought to bear. He must inspire confidence in air crews and know their ability and limitations. The good leader will aim to achieve a decisive success with the whole force under his command rather than gain personal victory.

Surprise is a most important factor in air fighting and a leader should maneuver for position to achieve surprise before attacking, if possible. Surprise may be achieved by –

Attacking from directly out of the sun,

Making use of the bank of haze. Aircraft approaching on the same level are difficult to see if they attack from the side remote from the sun. (A bomber, therefore, should try to fly well above the haze level so as to render a concealed approach by fighters less likely.)

In the evening or early morning by attacking from that part of the sky which is darker,

By making good use of clouds or, in the case of fighters, by making an intelligent estimate of where enemy aircraft is likely to emerge.

When an enemy aircraft is sighted in one direction, vigilance in other directions must not be relaxed. More often than not, other supporting aircraft will be in the vicinity. To launch blithely into the attack on the first enemy seen without a quick search for other enemy planes is a sure way to be shot out of the sky and never know what hit you.

SOME DO'S AND DON'TS

BEFORE taking off or landing, search the sky for enemy aircraft. It is at these moments your aircraft is most vulnerable.

If you hear gunfire, or see bullets hitting close to you or observe tracers going past, immediately take evasive action – then look around. Don't try too look before starting to turn. It might be too late.

Develop a rubber neck. Keep the sky under constant surveillance.

Watch your tail

Conserve ammunition.

Never fly or dive straight when being attacked by aircraft or anti-aircraft fire.

Fighters should endeavor not to close in on the enemy at too high a speed during the final stage of the approach or the burst of fire will be too short to be effective, or you may over-shoot altogether.

Don't go into the middle of a V of enemy bombers. Attack them from the flank, and from both flanks simultaneously, where possible.

When you are going into the attack, don't give the enemy a chance at a deflection shot at you. As far as you can, keep your nose on the enemy and approach from his blind spots when possible.

In attacking enemy bombers, don't fire a long burst if enemy fighters are about; two seconds is long enough. Then break away quickly and look about to be sure no enemy fighter is after you. If all is clear, you can take another crack at the bombers, if necessary.

Don't break away in a climbing turn. This gives an easy shot to the enemy rear gunner.

Don't leave your formation, if you can help it, unless ordered to do so.

Don't ever fly straight, especially if you are alone. Keep that rubber neck turning continuously and keep a lookout behind.

Don't let the enemy slip out of the sun to get you. In looking toward the sun, place a finger or thumb before your eyes.

Don't waste ammunition by firing at long ranges.

FORMATION PRINCIPLES

SIZE:

A large formation is more vulnerable to A. A. fire than a number of small formations.

The larger the formation, the less maneuverable it becomes. However, it is more likely to subject attacking aircraft to a superior concentration of fire.

With a large formation, there will be a tendency for a number of gunners to fire on a few enemy aircraft and to ignore others, and to waste ammunition. There is, therefore, a limit to the size of a formation to obtain economical fire concentration.

Aircraft which have blind sectors, or sectors of reduced fire power, need larger formations than those which have all around arcs of fire.

Small formations are less easily seen than large ones.

SHAPE:

Every pilot must be able easily to see the aircraft on which he is forming.

All aircraft in the formation must keep station on the leader, and as few as possible in sequence. Otherwise accumulated errors build up and the rearmost pilots have a very difficult task in maintaining proper position.

While being attacked, make it impossible to draw a straight line from the enemy's line of approach through two or more aircraft in the formation. Otherwise the attackers may successfully enfilade the formation.

The length of the formation should be equal in all directions, where possible.

All aircraft in the formation, with the possible exception of the leader, should be equidistant from the enemy aircraft. Thus, in defensive bomber formations, every aircraft will be spread perpendicular to the enemy's line of approach.

Aircraft in formation should be sufficiently far apart to avoid one plane being hit by shots aimed at the other. At the same time they must be sufficiently close to provide maximum mutual support.

Formations disposed in depths create a large volume of slipstream turbulence which, when bombers are being attacked from rear, throws fighters off their line of sight.

The ideal defensive formation will differ with every method and direction of attack. Each formation must, therefore, possess sufficient flexibility to allow a quick alteration to some other formation.

The disposition of aircraft in formation will depend upon circumstances. For example, if attack on a defensive bomber formation is developing from above, aircraft in the formation should be stepped down - if the attack is from below, the aircraft should be stepped up. If the attack is from the same level and developing from the beam, aircraft should be stepped down (for it is easier for fighters to sweep a formation UPWARDS than DOWNWARDS. With aircraft on the nearer flank DOWN and on the outer flank UP.)

When encountering A. A. fire all aircraft sections should be far enough apart to avoid more than one aircraft being brought down by any one A. A. burst.

EVASION PRINCIPLES

ALWAYS turn toward a fighter. Thus you shorten his approach, and therefore make him turn more rapidly. Maybe he won't be able, aerodynamically, to turn fast enough and he may be forced to break away. DO NOT turn away from the direction of attack.

A straight dive will give enemy aircraft a "sitting shot." You actually appear as a stationary target in such a dive either at a target plane or away from the plane.

Never change from one turn to a reverse turn. Wait for a brief interval between attacks. Take a quick look about before launching successive attacks.

When hedge hopping, or flying low over the sea, fly an erratic course.

Clouds, except the smallest ones, afford one the best means of avoiding enemy aircraft. When possible fly near the clouds, but if over areas covered by A. A. fire do not fly immediately below the cloud base, as A. A. can accurately determine the range from the cloud base.

Do not fly straight through a cloud when avoiding enemy aircraft. Alter the course in the cloud to turn towards the enemy.

Aircraft flying above 20,000 feet are difficult to see from the ground.

Avoid layers of air in which white streamers form astern.

At night do not open throttle because this increases length of exhaust flame which can be seen at long distances.

Show no lights on your aircraft.

Searchlight beams without accompanying A. A. fire indicate the presence of enemy fighters. Do everything possible to get out of the light.

To evade enemy fighters, fast bombers may be sent in advance of the striking force, to draw off enemy fighters. Also planes may be routed on dog-leg courses toward other important objectives with a view of deceiving the enemy as to the actual target.

EVADING SOUND LOCATORS

Searchlight and A. A. at night are directed by sound locators. (Radio aid is also said to be effective.) Sound locators may be avoided or deceived by one of the following means:

One aircraft to fly low, making a noise screen which will prevent aircraft flying high from being heard.

Gliding over the searchlight or A. A. belts in heights in excess of 6,000 feet where aircraft throttled back are inaudible.

Simultaneous raids on different or parallel courses at different heights will result in locators getting a false position.

Desynchronize engines. This is effective at least to inexperienced sound locator crews.

Most effective of all evasive measures are alternations in course, speed, and height.

Sound locator crews usually do not allow sufficiently for the lag in time it takes the engine noise to reach them which results in searchlights and A. A. fire being below and behind. (Recently it seems the German A. A. must be directed by radio-locators. Where radio-directed A. A. fire is encountered, some of the foregoing suggestions will not apply.)

In seeking to avoid searchlights, turn. A climb or dive, without a turn, is ineffective.

ANTI-AIRCRAFT EVASION

LONG RANGE A. A.

The A. A. gunner's greatest difficulty is finding the correct elevation. Consequently a change in height, as well as turning is the best method of evasion. Effective danger area of 3" and 4.5" shells is from 30 to 90 feet radius. The area behind and below the bursts is usually safe; therefore it is best to fly below shell bursts rather than above them.

When within range of enemy A. A., it is imperative that course and altitude be altered continuously to avoid destructive hits.

Heavy A. A. fire is most accurate between 6,000 and 18,000 feet; therefore, if possible, fly above or below these heights.

The ideal target from A. A. point of view as a large formation in line astern. The most difficult formation for A. A. are small sections (or 2 or 3) flying line abreast, or shallow echelon, at different heights

At night it has often proved effective to drop a flare, or other object, and then dive or climb in a turn. The enemy A. A. will often concentrate on the flare or object, and thus enable you to get away.

SHORT RANGE A. A.

Short range A. A. is usually ineffective at heights above 5,000 feet. Therefore fly at greater heights, or else very low.

Attacks against defended areas should be made suddenly and not repeated for at least five or ten minutes. Make a low and quick get-away without trying to manoeuver to observe effect of your attack.

Low flying attacks should be made from the direction of the sun, or from clouds and by taking advantage of topographical features.

If both short range and long range A. A. is expected, the best compromise is to fly at about 5,000 feet, at ground level, or above 18,000 feet.

SILHOUETTES AND SPECIFICATIONS

Aichi D3A "Val"

WING SPAN:	*33 feet, 1 1/2 inches*
LENGTH:	*33 feet, 5 1/2 inches*
HEIGHT:	*11 feet*
POWER:	*One Mitsubishi Kinsei 44 1070 h.p.*
WEIGHT:	*Empty: 5,309 pounds Loaded: 8,047 pounds*
MAXIMUM SPEED:	*242 m.p.h.*
SERVICE CEILING:	*31,170*

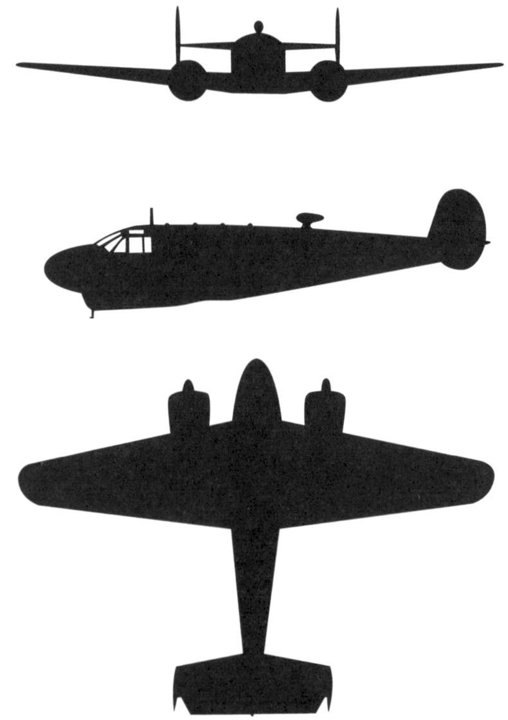

Beech C-45 "Expediter"

WING SPAN:	*47 feet, 8 inches*
LENGTH:	*34 feet, 3 inches*
HEIGHT:	*9 feet, 5 inches*
POWER:	*Two Pratt & Whitney Wasp Junior 450 h.p. each*
WEIGHT:	*Empty: 5,025 pounds Loaded: 7,500 pounds*
MAXIMUM SPEED:	*220 m.p.h.*
SERVICE CEILING:	*27,000 feet*
RANGE:	*1,000 miles*

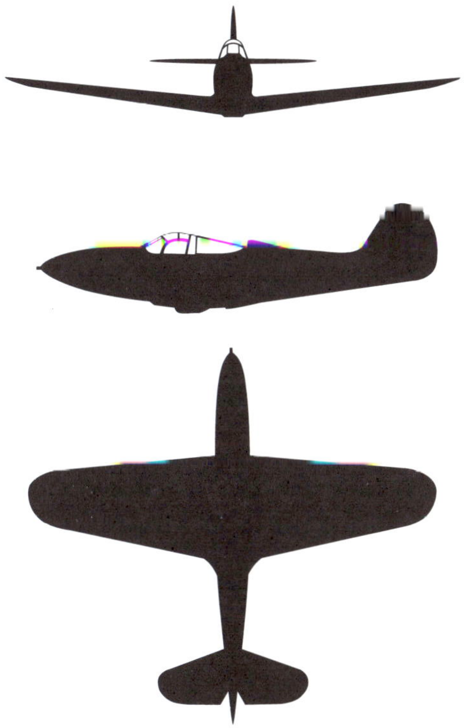

Bell P-39Q "Airacobra"

WING SPAN:	34 feet
LENGTH:	30 feet, 2 inches
HEIGHT:	12 feet, 5 inches
POWER:	One Allison V-1710-83 1,200 h.p.
WEIGHT:	Empty: 5,645 pounds Loaded: 8,300 pounds
MAXIMUM SPEED:	385 m.p.h.
SERVICE CEILING:	35,000 feet
RANGE:	1,250 miles

Bell P-63F "Kingcobra"

WING SPAN:	39 feet, 2 inches
LENGTH:	32 feet, 8 inches
HEIGHT:	12 feet, 9 inches
POWER	Allison V-1710-93 1,325 h.p.
WEIGHT:	Empty: 7300 pounds Loaded: 9400 pounds
MAXIMUM SPEED:	437 m.p.h.
SERVICE CEILING:	39,000 feet
RANGE:	2150 miles

Boeing B-17G "Flying Fortress"

WING SPAN:	*103 feet, 9 inches*
LENGTH:	*74 feet, 9 inches*
HEIGHT:	*19 feet, 1 inches*
POWER:	*Four Wright R-1820-97* *1,200 h.p. each*
WEIGHT:	*Empty: 36,135 pounds* *Loaded: 65,500 pounds*
MAXIMUM SPEED:	*287 m.p.h.*
SERVICE CEILING:	*35,600 feet*
RANGE:	*3,400 miles*

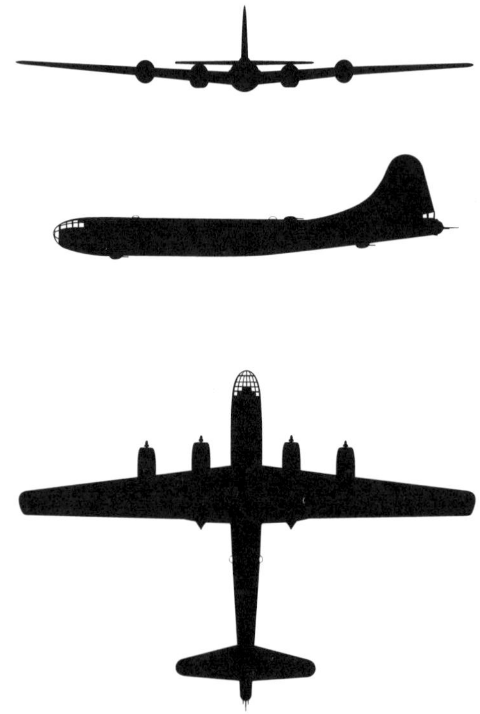

Boeing B-29 "Superfortress"

WING SPAN:	*141 feet, 3 inches*
LENGTH:	*99 feet*
HEIGHT:	*29 feet, 7 inches*
POWER:	*Four Wright R-3350-57* *2,200 h.p. each*
WEIGHT:	*Empty: 74,000 pounds* *Loaded: 135,000 pounds*
MAXIMUM SPEED:	*357 m.p.h.*
SERVICE CEILING:	*31,850 feet*
RANGE:	*3,250 miles*

Consolidated B-24J "Liberator"

WING SPAN:	*110 feet*
LENGTH:	*67 feet, 2 inches*
HEIGHT:	*18 feet*
POWER:	*Four P&W R-1830-65* *1,200 h.p. each*
WEIGHT:	*Empty: 36,500 pounds* *Loaded: 71,200 pounds*
MAXIMUM SPEED:	*290 m.p.h.*
SERVICE CEILING:	*28,000 feet*
RANGE:	*2,100 miles*

Consolidated PBY "Catalina"

WING SPAN:	*104 feet*
LENGTH:	*63 feet, 10 inches*
HEIGHT:	*20 feet, 2 inches*
POWER:	*Two Pratt & Whitney R-1830-92* *1,200 h.p. each*
WEIGHT:	*Empty: 20,910 pounds* *Loaded: 35,420 pounds*
MAXIMUM SPEED:	*179 m.p.h.*
SERVICE CEILING:	*14,700 feet*
RANGE:	*2,545 miles*

Curtiss C-46 "Commando"

WING SPAN:	*108 feet, 1 inch*
LENGTH:	*76 feet, 4 inches*
HEIGHT:	*21 feet, 9 inches*
POWER:	*Two Pratt & Whitney R-2800-51* *2,000 h.p. each*
WEIGHT:	*Empty: 32,400 pounds* *Loaded: 56,000 pounds*
MAXIMUM SPEED:	*269 m.p.h.*
SERVICE CEILING:	*27,600 feet*
RANGE:	*1,200 miles*

Curtiss P-40N "Kittyhawk"

WING SPAN:	*37 feet, 4 inches*
LENGTH:	*33 feet, 4 inches*
HEIGHT:	*12 feet, 4 inches*
POWER:	*One Allison V-1710-81* *1,200 h.p.*
WEIGHT:	*Empty: 6,200 pounds* *Loaded: 8,850 pounds*
MAXIMUM SPEED:	*343 m.p.h.*
SERVICE CEILING:	*31,000 feet*
RANGE:	*1,080 miles*

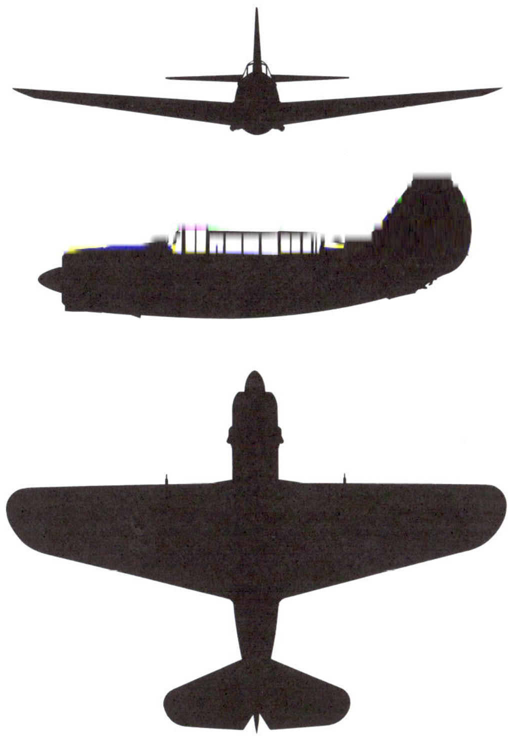

Curtiss SB2C-5 "Helldiver"

WING SPAN:	*49 feet, 9 inches*
LENGTH:	*36 feet, 8 inches*
HEIGHT:	*13 feet, 2 inches*
POWER:	*One Wright R-2600-20 1,900 h.p.*
WEIGHT:	*Empty: 10,589 pounds Loaded: 16,287 pounds*
MAXIMUM SPEED:	*290 m.p.h.*
SERVICE CEILING:	*27,600 feet*
RANGE:	*1,324 miles*

Douglas A-20 "Havoc"

WING SPAN:	*61 feet, 4 inches*
LENGTH:	*48 feet*
HEIGHT:	*17 feet, 7 inches*
POWER:	*Two Wright R-2600-23 Cyclone 1,600 each*
WEIGHT:	*Empty: 15,984 pounds Loaded: 27,200 pounds*
MAXIMUM SPEED:	*317 m.p.h.*
SERVICE CEILING:	*25,000 feet*
RANGE:	*1,025 miles*

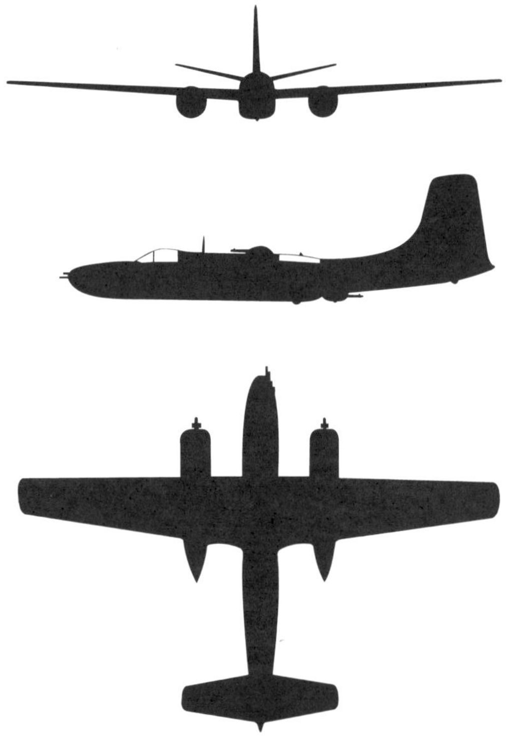

Douglas A-26B "Invader"

WING SPAN:	*70 feet*
LENGTH:	*50 feet*
HEIGHT:	*18 feet, 6 inches*
POWER:	*Two Pratt & Whitney R-2800-27* *2,000 h.p. each*
WEIGHT:	*Empty: 22,370 pounds* *Loaded: 35,000 pounds*
MAXIMUM SPEED:	*355 m.p.h.*
SERVICE CEILING:	*22,100 feet*
RANGE:	*1,400 miles*

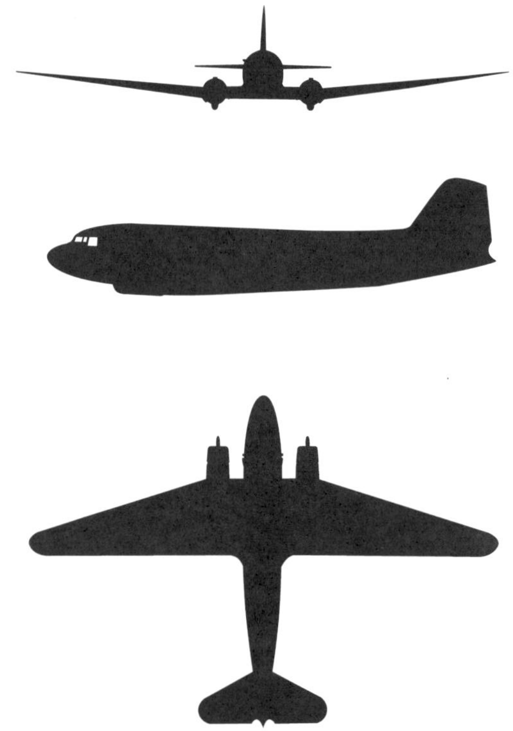

Douglas C-47 "Skytrain"

WING SPAN:	*95 feet*
LENGTH:	*64 feet, 6 inches*
HEIGHT:	*16 feet, 11 inches*
POWER:	*Two Pratt & Whitney R-1830* *1,200 h.p. each*
WEIGHT:	*Empty: 17,900 pounds* *Loaded: 26,900 pounds*
MAXIMUM SPEED:	*229 m.p.h.*
SERVICE CEILING:	*23,200 feet*
RANGE:	*1,500 miles*

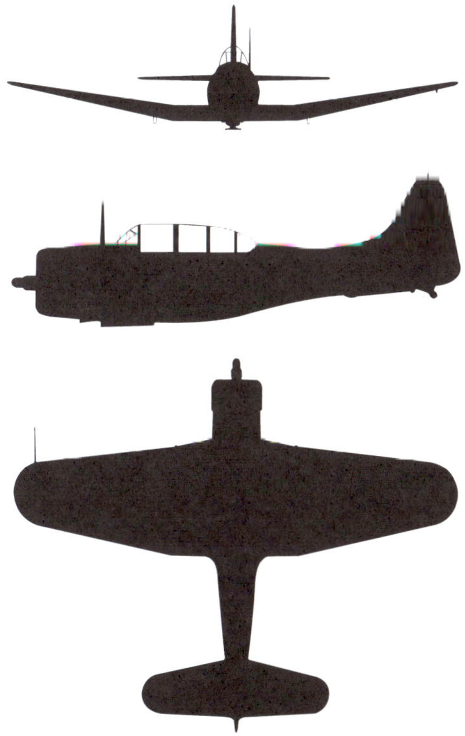

Douglas SBD-3 "Dauntless"

WING SPAN:	*41 feet, 6 1/4 inches*
LENGTH:	*33 feet, 1/8 inch*
HEIGHT:	[illegible]
POWER:	*One Wright R-1820* *1,000 h.p.*
WEIGHT:	*Empty: 6675 pounds* *Loaded: 10,855 pounds*
MAXIMUM SPEED:	*245 m.p.h. @ 15,800 feet*
SERVICE CEILING:	*24,300 feet*
RANGE:	*1100 miles*

Fieseler Fi-156-D "Storch"

WING SPAN:	*46 feet, 9 inches*
LENGTH:	*32 feet, 5 3/4 inches*
HEIGHT:	*10 feet*
POWER:	*Argus As 10C* *270 h.p.*
WEIGHT:	*Empty: 2050 pounds* *Loaded: 3498 pounds*
MAXIMUM SPEED:	*109 m.p.h.*
MINIMUM SPEED:	*32 m.p.h.*
SERVICE CEILING:	*19,358 feet*
RANGE:	*205 miles*

Grumman F4F-8 "Wildcat" (FM-2)

WING SPAN:	*38 feet*
LENGTH:	*28 feet, 11 inches*
HEIGHT:	*11 feet, 5 inches*
POWER:	*One Wright R-1820-56* *1,350 h.p.*
WEIGHT:	*Empty: 5,448 pounds* *Loaded: 8,271 pounds*
MAXIMUM SPEED:	*332 m.p.h.*
SERVICE CEILING:	*34,700 feet*
RANGE:	*1,310 miles*

Grumman F6F-5 "Hellcat"

WING SPAN:	*42 feet, 10 inches*
LENGTH:	*33 feet, 7 inches*
HEIGHT:	*11 feet, 5 inches*
POWER:	*One Pratt & Whitney R-2800-10W* *1,350 h.p.*
WEIGHT:	*Empty: 9,238 pounds* *Loaded: 15,413 pounds*
MAXIMUM SPEED:	*380 m.p.h.*
SERVICE CEILING:	*37,300 feet*
RANGE:	*1,355 miles*

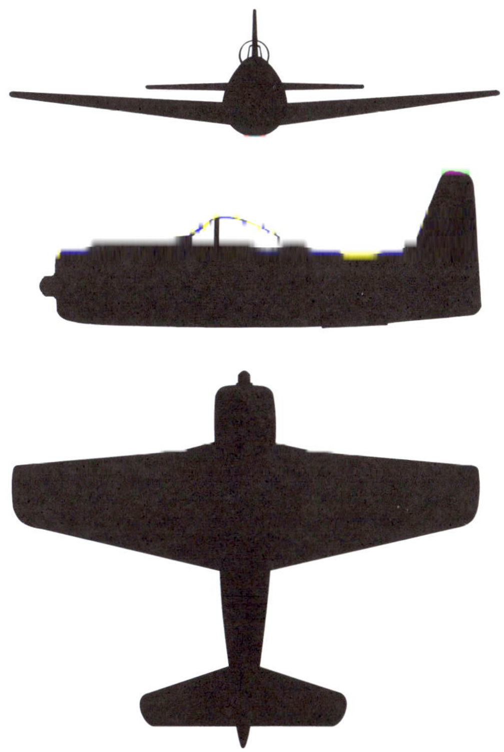

Grumman F8F-2 "Bearcat"

WING SPAN:	*35 feet, 6 inches*
LENGTH:	*27 feet 8 inches*
HEIGHT:	*12 feet, 2 inches*
POWER:	*One Pratt & Whitney R-2000-34W 2,300 h.p.*
WEIGHT:	*Empty: 7,690 pounds Loaded: 13,494 pounds*
MAXIMUM SPEED:	*447 m.p.h.*
SERVICE CEILING:	*40,700 feet*
RANGE:	*1,435 miles*

Grumman (General Motors) TBM-3 "Avenger"

WING SPAN:	*54 feet, 2 inches*
LENGTH:	*40 feet*
HEIGHT:	*16 feet, 5 inches*
POWER:	*Wright R-2600-20 1,900 h.p.*
WEIGHT:	*Empty: 10,843 pounds Loaded: 18,250 pounds*
MAXIMUM SPEED:	*267 m.p.h.*
SERVICE CEILING:	*23,400 feet*
RANGE:	*2,335 miles*

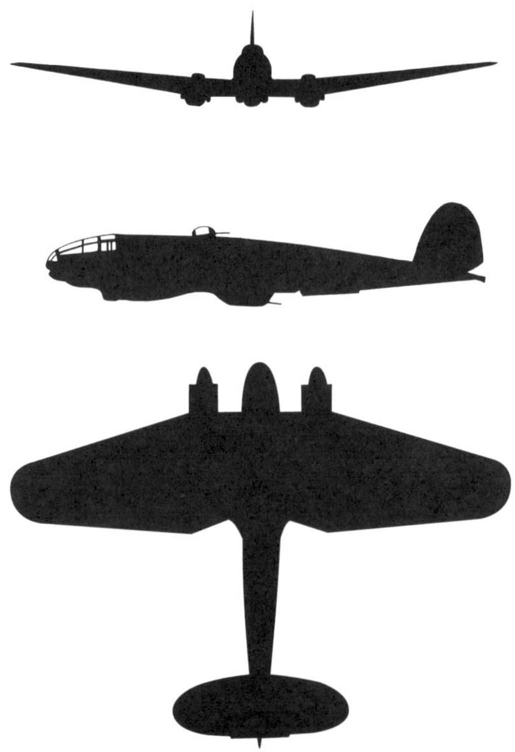

Heinkel He111

WING SPAN:	*74 feet, 1 1/2 inches*
LENGTH:	*54 feet, 5 1/2 inches*
HEIGHT:	*13 feet, 8 inches*
POWER:	*Two Junkers Jumo 211F-2s 1,340 h.p. each*
WEIGHT:	*Empty: 14,400 pounds Loaded: 27,400 pounds*
MAXIMUM SPEED:	*258 m.p.h.*
SERVICE CEILING:	*25,500 feet*
RANGE:	*1,740 miles*

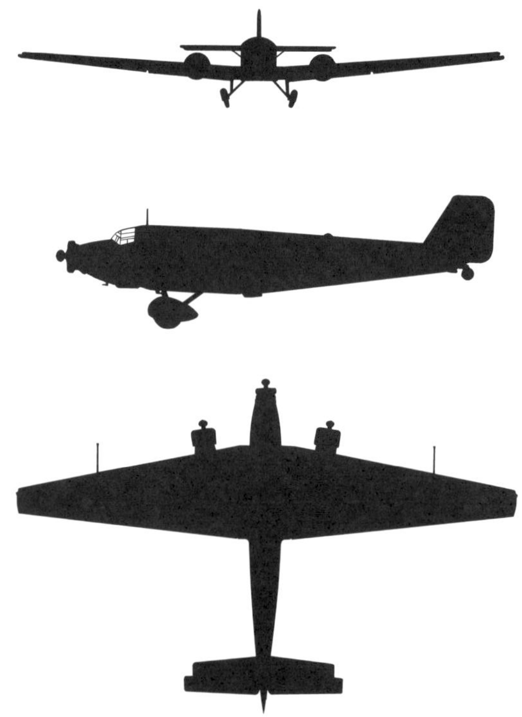

Junkers Ju-52

WING SPAN:	*95 feet, 11 1/2 inches*
LENGTH:	*62 feet*
HEIGHT:	*18 feet, 2 1/2 inches*
POWER:	*Three BMW 132A-3 725 h.p. each*
WEIGHT:	*Empty: 12,610 pounds Loaded: 23,146 pounds*
MAXIMUM SPEED:	*172 m.p.h.*
SERVICE CEILING:	*19,360 feet*
RANGE:	*620 miles*

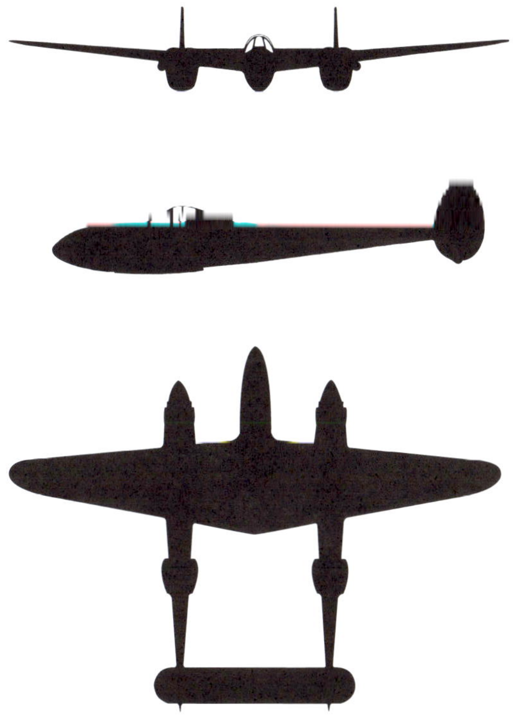

Lockheed P-38J "Lightning"

WING SPAN:	*52 feet*
LENGTH:	*37 feet, 10 inches*
HEIGHT:	*[illegible] feet, [illegible] inches*
POWER:	*Two Allison V-1710-89* *1,425 h.p. each*
WEIGHT:	*Empty: 12,800 pounds* *Loaded: 21,600 pounds*
MAXIMUM SPEED:	*414 m.p.h.*
SERVICE CEILING:	*44,000 feet*
RANGE:	*1,600 miles*

Martin B-26G "Marauder"

WING SPAN:	*71 feet*
LENGTH:	*56 feet, 1 inches*
HEIGHT:	*20 feet, 4 inches*
POWER:	*Two Pratt & Whitney R-2800-43* *1,920 h.p. each*
WEIGHT:	*Empty: 25,300 pounds* *Loaded: 38,200 pounds*
MAXIMUM SPEED:	*283 m.p.h.*
SERVICE CEILING:	*19,800 feet*
RANGE:	*1,100 miles*

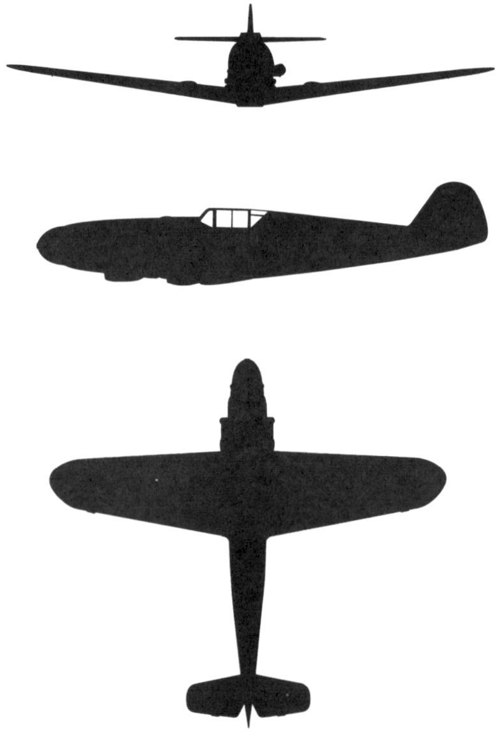

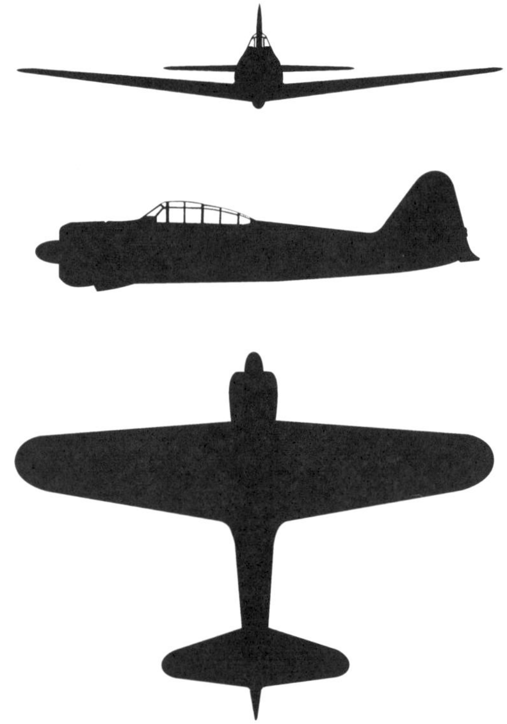

MESSERSCHMITT Bf109E-4

WING SPAN:	*32 feet, 4 1/2 inches*
LENGTH:	*28 feet, 4 1/4 inches*
HEIGHT:	*8 feet, 2 1/5 inches*
POWER:	*Daimler-Benz DB 601A 1,100 h.p.*
WEIGHT:	*Empty: 4,360 pounds Loaded: 5,400 pounds*
MAXIMUM SPEED:	*354 @ 12,300 feet*
SERVICE CEILING:	*36,000 feet*
RANGE:	*412 miles @ 16,400 feet*

Mitsubishi A6M5 "Zero"

WING SPAN:	*36 feet, 1 inch*
LENGTH:	*29 feet, 9 inches*
HEIGHT:	*9 feet, 2 inches*
POWER:	*One Nakajima Sakae 21 1,130 h.p.*
WEIGHT:	*Empty: 3,920 pounds Loaded: 6.508 pounds*
MAXIMUM SPEED:	*358 m.p.h.*
SERVICE CEILING:	*35,100 feet*
RANGE:	*1,130 miles*

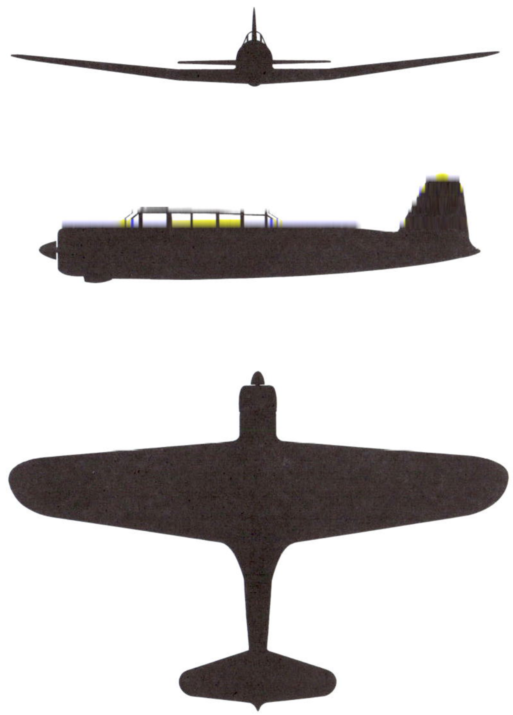

Nakajima B5N "Kate"

WING SPAN:	*50 feet, 11 inches*
LENGTH:	*33 feet, 10 inches*
HEIGHT:	*12 feet, 2 inches*
POWER:	*One Sakae 11 1,000 h.p.*
WEIGHT:	*Empty: 4,830 pounds Loaded: 8,360 pounds*
MAXIMUM SPEED:	*235 m.p.h.*
SERVICE CEILING:	*25,200 feet*
RANGE:	*1,238 miles*

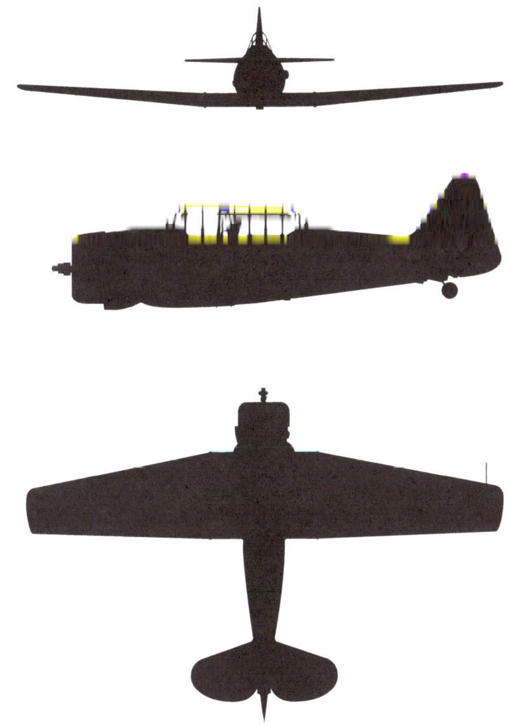

North American AT-6 "Texan"

WING SPAN:	*42 feet*
LENGTH:	*29 feet, 6 inches*
HEIGHT:	*11 feet, 8 inches*
POWER:	*One Pratt & Whitney "Wasp" 550 h.p.*
WEIGHT:	*Empty: 4,106 pounds Loaded: 5,248 pounds*
MAXIMUM SPEED:	*208 m.p.h.*
SERVICE CEILING:	*24,200 feet*
RANGE:	*750 miles*

North American B-25D "Mitchell"

WING SPAN:	*67 feet, 7 inches*
LENGTH:	*52 feet, 11 inches*
HEIGHT:	*16 feet, 4 inches*
POWER:	*Two Wright R-2600-13* *1,700 each*
WEIGHT:	*Empty: 29,500 pounds* *Loaded: 41,800 pounds*
MAXIMUM SPEED:	*272 m.p.h.*
SERVICE CEILING:	*25,000 feet*
RANGE:	*1,275 miles*

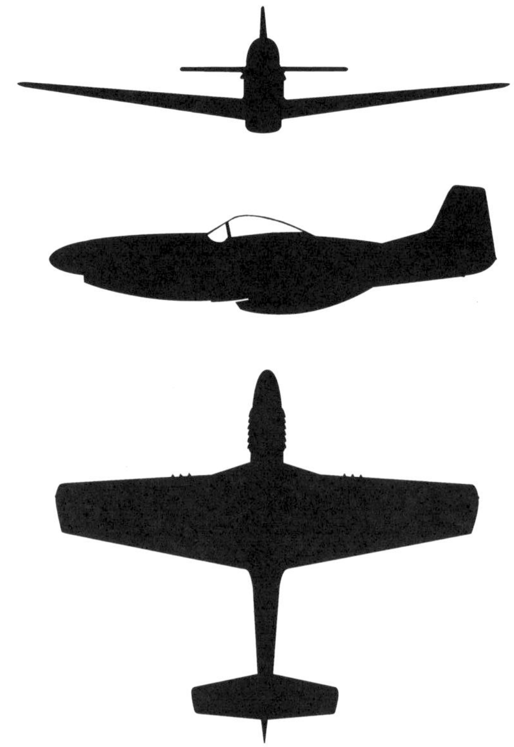

North American P-51D "Mustang"

WING SPAN:	*37 feet*
LENGTH:	*32 feet, 3 inches*
HEIGHT:	*13 feet, 8 inches*
POWER:	*Packard V-1650-7* *1,695 h.p.*
WEIGHT:	*Empty: 7,125 pounds* *Loaded: 12,100 pounds*
MAXIMUM SPEED:	*437 m.p.h.*
SERVICE CEILING:	*41,900 feet*
RANGE:	*2,080 miles (external tanks)*

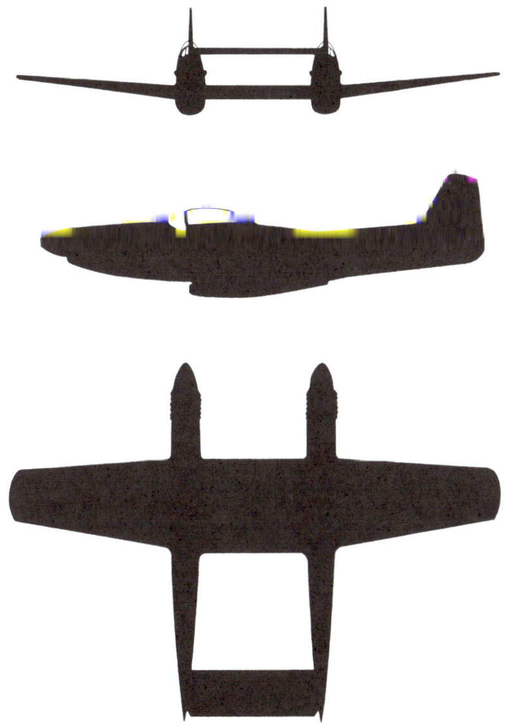

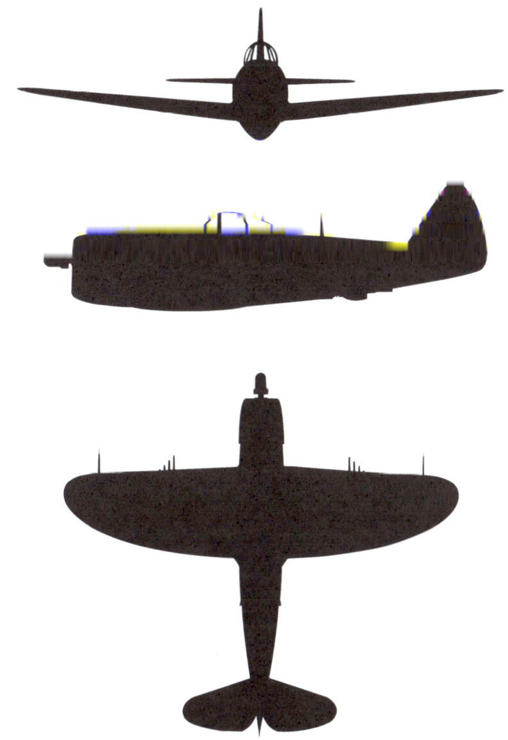

North American P-82B "Twin Mustang"

WING SPAN:	*51 feet, 3 inches*
LENGTH:	*39 feet, 1 inch*
HEIGHT:	*13 feet, 10 inch*
POWER:	*Two Allison V-1710-143/145* *1,600 h.p. each*
WEIGHT:	*Empty: 14,914 pounds* *Loaded: 24,813 pounds*
MAXIMUM SPEED:	*465 m.p.h.*
SERVICE CEILING:	*40,000 feet*
RANGE:	*2,504 miles*

Republic P-47D "Thunderbolt"

WING SPAN:	*40 feet, 9 inches*
LENGTH:	*[illegible] feet, [illegible] inches*
HEIGHT:	*14 feet, 2 inches*
POWER:	*One Pratt & Whitney R-2800-59* *2,535 h.p.*
WEIGHT:	*Empty: 11,000* *Loaded: 19,400 pounds*
MAXIMUM SPEED:	*428 m.p.h.*
SERVICE CEILING:	*42,000 feet*
RANGE:	*475 miles*

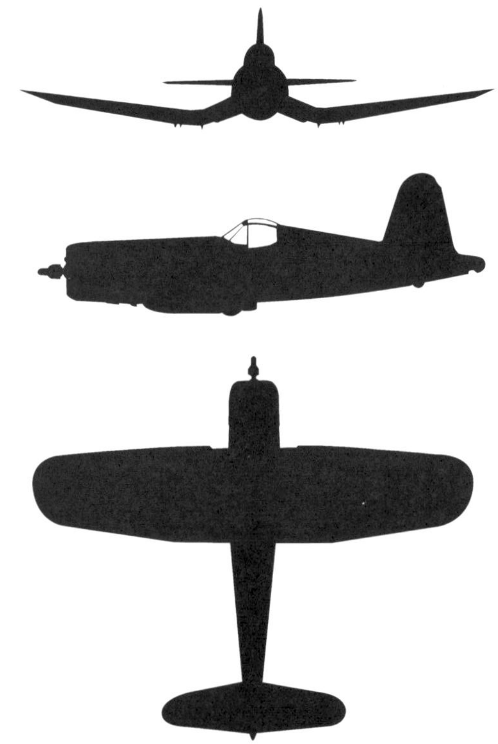

Supermarine "Spitfire" Mk. IX

WING SPAN:	*36 feet, 10 inches*
LENGTH:	*31 feet*
HEIGHT:	*11 feet, 5 inches*
POWER:	*One Rolls-Royce "Merlin" 61* *1,515 h.p.*
WEIGHT:	*Loaded: 7,300 pounds*
MAXIMUM SPEED:	*408 m.p.h.*
SERVICE CEILING:	*44,000 feet*
RANGE:	*434 miles*

Vought/Goodyear FG-1D "Corsair"

WING SPAN:	*41 feet*
LENGTH:	*34 feet, 6 inches*
HEIGHT:	*14 feet, 9 inches*
POWER:	*One Pratt & Whitney R-2800* *2,300 h.p.*
WEIGHT:	*Empty: 9,683 pounds* *Loaded: 14,106 pounds*
MAXIMUM SPEED:	*470 m.p.h.*
SERVICE CEILING:	*41,600 feet*
RANGE:	*1,120 miles*

Addendum

THE AIRCRAFT OF THE CONFEDERATE AIR FORCE

N NUMBER	AIRCRAFT TYPE	CONFEDERATE AIRFORCE WING OR SQUADRON
101X	*SNJ-5*	HIGH SKY WING
10601	*P-51*	COL RICK SHARPE
1078Z	*F8F*	COL BRUCE LOCKWOOD
109ME	*ME-109*	COL DAN LAWSON
11171	*AT-6B*	GULF COAST WING
1156V	*L-5*	NATIONAL CAPITAL SQD
12102	*P-82*	P-82 SQD
1226N	*P-40*	COL OLLIE CRAWFORD
1238N	*T-50*	HEADQUARTERS
125AZ	*B-25*	ARIZONA WING
13595	*HARVARD MK IV*	SO MINNESOTA WING
1387V	*PT-17*	UTAH WING
145AZ	*C-45*	ARIZONA WING
151ZE	*R4D*	DFW WING
1553V	*JRB-4*	HEADQUARTERS
15797	*HARVARD MK IV*	GULF COAST WING
15799	*HARVARD MK IV*	GULF COAST WING
16BR	*FLEET*	RGV WING
191H	*P-63*	DIXIE WING
19GH	*O2-A*	ARIZONA WING
1VC	*MIG 17*	GOLDEN GATE WING
2047	*HARVARD MK IV*	COL BILL POWERS
215CA	*P-51*	SO MINNESOTA WING
2231	*ME-108*	NEW MEXICO WING
224X	*SNJ-4*	CLEVELAND WING
227GB	*C-47*	GREAT LAKES WING
22AL	*PT-22*	RGV WING
2354H	*YO-55*	BIG THICKET WING
240P	*A-26*	RANGER WING
24927	*B-24/LB30*	B-29 SQD
2497	*FW-44*	RGV WING
25462	*UC-94*	BIG COUNTRY SQD
2581B	*L-5*	KEYSTONE WING
25YR	*B-25*	YELLOW ROSE SQD
26GA	*PT-26*	DIXIE WING
26295	*L-9B*	KEYSTONE WING
27003	*BT-13*	WEST HOUSTON SQD
27493	*B-25*	SO MINNESOTA WING
27933	*PT-17*	LONE STAR WING
2995C	*L-17*	FLORIDA WING
30N	*C-60*	OLD DOMINION SQD
3195G	*SNJ-5*	GOLDEN GATE WING
320A	*AT-11*	WEST MICHIGAN WING
3246G	*SNJ-5*	ARIZONA WING
324FA	*28-5ACF (PBY)*	SO MINNESOTA WING
3481G	*B-25*	MISSOURI WING
352JU	*JU-52*	GREAT LAKES WING
35786	*L-4*	INLAND EMPIRE WING
36681	*L-3S*	MISSOURI WING
36687	*L-3E*	GREAT PLAINS WING
3725G	*SNJ-5*	GULF COAST WING
38LL	*P-38*	HEADQUARTERS
40FS	*FI-156*	HILL COUNTRY SQD
40074	*C-45*	CIMARRON STRIP WING
40402	*TBM-3E*	STARS & STRIPES WING
4207	*C-45*	MISSISSIPPI WING
444AC	*L-17*	HIGHLAND LAKES
4447	*HARVARD MK IV*	GULF COAST WING
44741	*N3N*	WEST HOUSTON SQD
44795	*UC-78*	JAYHAWK WING
4574Y	*BT-14 NA-64*	HEADQUARTERS
46336	*L-6*	DELAWARE VALLEY SQD
46337	*L-6*	HEADQUARTERS
46693	*PT-26*	RGV WING
46876	*PT-19*	SPRIT OF TULSA WING
47TB	*P-47*	COL DOUG JEANES
4732G	*PT-26*	RGV WING
48742	*PT-22*	INLAND EMPIRE WING
50481	*PT-19*	HEART OF AMERICA
5138B	*OY-2*	OHIO VALLEY WING
519SH	*PT-26*	OKLAHOMA WING
52411	*BT-13A*	SO MINNESOTA WING
5264V	*TBM-3*	MISSOURI WING
529B	*B-29*	B-29 SQD
53503	*TBM-3*	ROCKY MOUNTAIN WING

N NUMBER	AIRCRAFT TYPE	CONFEDERATE AIRFORCE WING OR SQUADRON	N NUMBER	AIRCRAFT TYPE	CONFEDERATE AIRFORCE WING OR SQUADRON	N NUMBER	AIRCRAFT TYPE	CONFEDERATE AIRFORCE WING OR SQUADRON
53594	*C-46*	SO CALIFORNIA WING	64176	*PT-23*	JAYHAWK WING	7825C	*F8F*	SO CALIFORNIA WING
53768	*L-2*	EVERGREEN WING	64513	*T-50*	COL JACK CRIST	78774	*C-46*	C-46 COMMANDO SQD
5420V	*P-51*	COL REG URSCHLER	65494	*AT-11*	HEADQUARTERS	[illegible]	*C-45*	NEW MEXICO WING
[illegible]	[illegible]	[illegible] WING	[illegible]	[illegible]	[illegible]	[illegible]	[illegible]	[illegible] WING
5625V	*L-5E*	CENTRAL CA VALLEY	66681	*BT-13A*	BIG THICKET WING	81348	*UC-61*	HIGH SKY WING
56360	*BT-13A*	NATIONAL CAPITAL SQD	66791	*BT-13A*	HIGH SKY WING	82GA	*SBD*	DIXIE WING
56478	*BT-13*	GULF COAST WING	67208	*BT-13*	GULF COAST WING	86493	*PV-2*	WISCONSIN WING
57789	*L-5*	DFW WING	67227	*AT-19*	NEVADA WING	89014	*SNJ-5*	SO CALIFORNIA WING
58123	*PT-19*	HIGH SKY WING	6725	*UH-19D*	ARIZONA WING	89605	*C-140*	SO CALIFORNIA WING
58245	*A6M2*	COL DAVID PRICE	6763	*P-63*	COL SCOTT ROZZELL	90SQ	*WOLF*	HEADQUARTERS
5833	*FM-2*	COL BOB REISS	681S	*FM-2*	COL BOB PETERS	9097	*HARVARD MK IV*	GULF COAST WING
5855	*C-45*	FLORIDA WING	68591	*L-5*	SO MINNESOTA WING	9124Z	*T-33*	GOLDEN GATE WING
5865V	*B-25*	SO CALIFORNIA WING	68756	*PBY-5A*	RGV WING	92879	*SB2C*	WEST TEXAS WING
59AF	*L-5*	AIR GROUP ONE	69605	*BT-15*	DFW WING	9315H	*L-5*	OLD DOMINION SQD
60535	*PT-26*	INDIANA WING	6968	*P-39*	CEN TEX WING	9323Z	*B-17*	ARIZONA WING
60634	*AT-19*	CAROLINAS WING	70GA	*C-45*	DIXIE WING	94DH	*DH-94*	RGV WING
6072C	*PT-26*	RAZORBACK WING	7024C	*SNJ-4*	COL HAROLD BROWN	96281	*HARVARD II*	3RD PURSUIT SQD
6125H	*J-3 CUB*	ROCKY MOUNTAIN WING	7058Q	*PT-17*	LONE STAR WING	9643C	*B-25*	DEVIL DOG SQD
61957	*DHC-1*	CHIPMUNK GROUP	70743	*T-28A*	HAWKEYE STATE SQD	9682C	*A-26*	COL DAN LAWSON
62G	*B-23*	HEADQUARTERS	7179Y	*PBY-6A*	SO MINNESOTA WING	97040	*S-108*	WEST HOUSTON SQD
626SH	*A-26*	S/H SPONSOR GROUP	7227C	*B-17*	GULF COAST WING	9790Z	*T-6*	WEST HOUSTON SQD
6371C	*L-18*	MILE HIGH WING	72615	*HE-111*	ARIZONA WING	9820C	*T-6*	GULF COAST WING
[illegible]	[illegible]	[illegible]	[illegible]	[illegible]	AIR GROUP ONE	[illegible]	[illegible]	[illegible]
[illegible]	*SNJ-4*	SO CALIFORNIA WING	[illegible]	[illegible]	ARIZONA WING	[illegible]	[illegible]	ARIZONA WING

THE WINGS AND SQUADRONS OF THE CONFEDERATE AIR FORCE

STATE/CITY	UNIT
ARIZONA, Mesa	Arizona Wing
ARKANSAS, Pine Bluff	Razorback Wing
CALIFORNIA, Camarillo	So California Wing
CALIFORNIA, Modesto/Oakdale	Central CA Valley Sqd
CALIFORNIA, Oakland	Golden Gate Wing
CALIFORNIA, Riverside	Inland Empire Wing
CALIFORNIA, San Diego	Air Group One Wing
CALIFORNIA, Upland	3rd Pursuit Squadron
COLORADO, Boulder	Mile High Wing
COLORADO, Grand Junction	Rocky Mountain Wing
FLORIDA, DeLand	Florida Wing
GEORGIA, Atlanta	Dixie Wing
ILLINOIS, Chicago	Great Lakes Wing
INDIANA, Anderson	Indiana Wing
IOWA, Ankeny	Hawkeye State Squadron
KANSAS, Kansas City	Heart of America Wing
KANSAS, Wichita	Jayhawk Wing
MARYLAND, Frederick	Stars & Stripes Wing
MICHIGAN, Grand Rapids	West Michigan Wing
MINNESOTA, So. Saint Paul	So Minnesota Wing
MISSISSIPPI, Madison	Mississippi Wing
MISSOURI, Springfield	Ozark Mountain Squadron
MISSOURI, St. Louis	Missouri Wing
NEBRASKA, Omaha	Great Plains Wing
NEVADA, Las Vegas	Nevada Wing
NEW MEXICO, Albuquerque	Lobo Wing
NEW MEXICO, Hobbs	New Mexico Wing
N. CAROLINA, Southern Pines	Carolinas Wing
OHIO, Cleveland	Cleveland Wing
OHIO, Columbus	Ohio Valley Wing

STATE/CITY	UNIT
OKLAHOMA, Guymon	Cimarron Strip Wing
OKLAHOMA, Oklahoma City	Oklahoma Wing
OKLAHOMA, Tulsa	Spirit Of Tulsa Squadron
PENNSYLVANIA, Philadelphia	Delaware Valley Wing
PENNSYLVANIA, Pittsburgh	Keystone Wing
TEXAS, Abilene	Big Country Squadron
TEXAS, Boerne	Hill Country Squadron
TEXAS, Brownsville	Rio Grande Valley Wing
TEXAS, Burnet	Highland Lakes Squadron
TEXAS, Conroe	Big Thicket Squadron
TEXAS, Corpus Christi	3rd Coast Squadron
TEXAS, Corsicana	Coyote Squadron
TEXAS, Dallas/Ft. Worth	Dallas/Ft. Worth Wing
TEXAS, Graham	Cactus Squadron
TEXAS, Houston	Gulf Coast Wing
TEXAS, Houston	West Houston Squadron
TEXAS, Marshall	Lone Star Wing
TEXAS, Midland	High Sky Wing
TEXAS, Midland	West Texas Wing
TEXAS, Odessa	Desert Squadron
TEXAS, Pampa	Dew Line Squadron
TEXAS, San Marcos	Centex Wing
TEXAS, San Marcos	Yellow Rose Squadron
TEXAS, Waco	Ranger Wing
UTAH, Salt Lake City	Utah Wing
VIRGINIA, Chesapeake	Old Dominion Squadron
VIRGINIA, Manassas	National Capitol Squadron
WASHINGTON, Seattle	Evergreen Wing
WISCONSIN, Milwaukee	Wisconsin Wing

AIRCRAFT SUPPORT SQUADRONS

B-26 Squadron
B-29/B-24 Squadron
C-46 Commando Composite Squadron
Devil Dog Squadron
P-82 Squadron
Training Detachment One

SPECIAL INTEREST UNITS

AIRSHO Support Detachment
Culpeper's Angels
Explosives Ordnance Detachment
Medical Detachment
Security Detachment

FOREIGN SUPPORTERS

AUSTRALIA	Australian Wing
FRANCE	French Supporter Squadron
NEW ZEALAND	South Pacific Wing
SWITZERLAND	Swiss Supporter Squadron

HEADQUARTERS of the CONFEDERATE AIR FORCE

PO BOX 62000
9600 WRIGHT DRIVE
MIDLAND, TX 79711-2000
(915) 563-1000